WILLIAM G. SMITH

Triumph
of the Pawns

Tales of an American Family
Imprisoned in Manila in World War II

novum ▰ premium

This book is also available as e-book.

www.novumpublishing.com

© 2020 novum publishing

ISBN 978-1-64268-189-5
Editing: Karen Simmering
Cover photo: William G. Smith
Cover design, layout & typesetting: novum publishing
Internal illustrations: William G. Smith

www.novumpublishing.com

For Mary Alice ...

And Liz, because she asked

Introduction

*The Chinese have a **curse**: "May you live in interesting times."*

Any person's life can be "cursed" by the times in which they live. But it is also true that a life is often shaped more by the people one lives with and how they react to their circumstances than it is by actual events themselves.

I think these stories are interesting, focusing as they do on the people interned by the Japanese in the Philippine Islands. The tales are not directly mine, but are a kind of oral history—the memories of others, primarily my parents, passed at the dinner table, in conversations with friends, or as reminiscences spoken of quietly (or often with humor), which became part of our lives, as Santo Tomas Internment Camp in Manila was part of our lives from 1941–1945.

The tales are personal—the experiences of normal people in abnormal circumstances. They are important because together they form a picture of a unique American historical event generally not well-known today: namely, the largest imprisonment of American civilians by a foreign power in the country's history.

Certainly, I was part of this, being born in the internment camp. But I participated much later on as an eager novitiate sitting and listening to the stories of my past as they were told and retold. These are my memories of the memories of my parents, the Foleys, my grandparents, family, and other internees we saw from time to time who knew parts and pieces. Plus, information from letters, telegrams, a chronology kept by my mother, excerpts of a speech made by Mary Alice Foley to the U.S. Army 1ˢᵗ Cavalry Division at their 50th Commemoration in 1994 of the liberation of the Philippines, and other material mostly tucked away in a big manila envelope by my grandmother, Annie Bishop.

Additional information, statistics, and background were derived from A. V. H. Hartendorp's The SantoTomas Story *(McGraw-Hill, 1964); J.E. McCall's* Santo Tomas Internment Camp *(The Woodruff Printing Co., 1945);* The Battle for Manila *by Connaughton, Pimlott and Anderson (Presidio Press, 1995);* Surviving a Japanese P.O.W. Camp *by Peter Wygle (Pathfinder Publishing of California, 1991);* Captured *by Frances B. Cogan (University of Georgia Press, 2000),* 100 Miles to Freedom *by Robert B. Holland (Turner Publishing Co., 2011);* The Mary Alice Foley Papers, *William L. Clements Library, The University of Michigan.*

To me, these stories were always interesting, especially the retelling of them over the years. I think they show why I have always felt I was blessed by the people around me—the pawns of war—much more than I was cursed by the situation we lived through. This work celebrates the internees and the brave, supportive Filipino people, all of whom should be remembered and their sacrifices never forgotten.

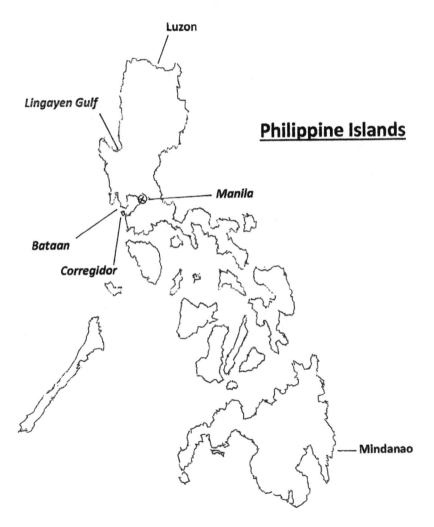

Formosa
(Taiwan)

Luzon

Lingayen Gulf

Philippine Islands

Manila

Bataan

Corregidor

Mindanao

May

May Birt Smith shuffled through the shoe box where she kept the prior year's Christmas cards. She found the one from the Bishops, mailed from Delaware last year, the parents and family of her eldest son's wife, none of whom she had ever met or even talked with. She set the card box on the kitchen table, picked up a pen to write, and then set it back down. She reached across and picked up the letter from the British Red Cross.

"Madame," it began. "We have been informed by British authorities that your son, Robert Elliott Smith, his wife Naomi, and their son, Robert B., are prisoners of the Japanese in Manila, the Philippine Islands. They are interned at Santo Tomas University in that city. No additional information is available at this time. As Mr. Smith is a British subject, His Majesty's Government has informed us that they will endeavor to do all possible to secure additional information as to his status and that of his family. Please address inquiries to this office. Recognizing that wartime conditions in London may delay replies, we request patience as we seek information through the International Red Cross and others, as well as from Japanese and British authorities in the East."

May was 57 years old, a petite, gray-haired woman with hazel green eyes. Her husband, Henry Robert, had died in a car-train accident in 1928 near Azusa, east of Los Angeles, where he was the pastor of the Citrus Baptist Church. He had been English-born, emigrating to America in 1891 at age 27 and settling in California, where he met his Missouri-born wife, May. They were married in Gardena in 1906. Although the Reverend Smith was a naturalized American citizen, the British still considered him British. Following their marriage, he and May, who was 21 years his junior, moved to Richmond, Indiana, to take up a post at the Baptist church there. Their first son, Robert, whom the British also considered British, was born in Richmond in 1908. A few years later, the family moved back to Southern California, where the Reverend Smith took up his ministry in the rural farming town of Azusa.

Orange groves, dairy cows, and field crops surrounded the small town, circled to the north by the sometimes-winter, snow-frosted San Gabriel Mountains. The son lived a bucolic childhood, herding dairy cows some mornings before school to make spending money, occasionally setting out smudge pots in the orange groves when frost threatened, and playing sports of course. Growing up, he played piano and organ in the church for no pay, and played organ accompanying the silent pictures at the local movie house for a dollar a night, an activity frowned on by the deacons of the church.

After the reverend's accident, May got a job at the May Co. department store in downtown Los Angeles, altering corsets for ladies on the fourth floor of the store. By 1942, she had worked there for nearly 13 years. It was a quiet life like that of most people.

But now, the three-month-old Japanese-American war was coming home. Only the week before, her second son, Gilbert H. Smith, some two years younger than Bob, had joined the Merchant Marine. He was in training in San Francisco. She had taken the unusual step of telephoning him the day before with the news of his brother Bob. It had been frightfully expensive to call all the way to San Francisco from Los Angeles, but she felt it was necessary.

May put down the letter and picked up her pen. "Dear Mr. and Mrs. Bishop," she began. "I don't know what you have been

11

told, but I received the following letter just yesterday." She copied out the message from the British Red Cross in her careful, neat handwriting. "If there is any news from your end, please let me know." She signed off "May Smith (your daughter's mother-in-law)," and added her address in Los Angeles. She sent it via air mail, another justifiable extravagance. It was the first word the Bishops had of their daughter. Nearly three weeks later, the American Red Cross sent a very similar letter to the Bishops, and later to May. The Bishops sent May an immediate return reply. May died in April 1947 in Los Angeles, and they never met.

The Beginning

Pre-war, in the 1930s, a slow boat to China was about the only way ordinary people could travel across the Pacific. The standard sailing schedule was pretty routine on one of a dozen ships, each some 500 feet in length, and all combining passenger and cargo services to try to maximize revenues. The well-to-do could take a Pan Am Clipper, the *Philippine Clipper* or the *China Clipper*, but the ticket cost almost as much as a new Chevrolet coupe. And in 1937, crawling through the seemingly endless Depression, few had that kind of money. So, for most people, the six-plus week trip by ocean liner, generally carrying a couple hundred passengers in three classes, was the common path: San Francisco to Honolulu, and then Yokohama, Kobe, Shanghai, Hong Kong, then Manila.

Naomi Bishop had three brothers. Her father, George C. Bishop, a college graduate and former teacher, believed in education and had sent her, the eldest child, to the University of Pennsylvania in Philadelphia, from which she graduated in 1927 and became a teacher. Her oldest brother, George H. Bishop, had gone to West Point, graduating in 1933, and was commissioned a second lieutenant. The other two boys, John and Bill, had graduated from the University of Delaware in 1936 and the University of Maryland in 1937 respectively. In between the two eldest and the two youngest, Naomi's father, George Bishop, had been hammered by the Depression and forced to declare bankruptcy for his lumber and timber distribution business. Due to Depression cutbacks, Naomi had lost her first teaching job at Glassboro Normal School, which was a secondary school in Glassboro, New Jersey, today known as Rowan University. She came home to live with her parents and was hired to teach in the local school just across the street from the family home in Laurel, Delaware, in the rural southwest corner of that small state. She paid for her younger two brothers' college educations as her father wrestled with repairing his business. With business conditions showing significant improvement in late 1936 and as a thank you, her father had given her a gift of a trip to visit her brother, George, a first lieutenant stationed with the U.S. Army in Manila. Her trip concluded with an extended return home around the world. American Express arranged for the whole thing—even the train from Philadelphia to San Francisco. She left Philadelphia after the June graduation in 1937 of her youngest brother, James William Bishop. She was just shy of her 32nd birthday.

Bob Smith had worked for the drug distribution and manufacturing firm McKesson & Robbins in Los Angeles from the early 1930s. A 1930 graduate in chemistry from Stanford University, Bob, like many others during the Depression, held tightly to his job while keeping an eye out for something better. One day, just a week after he returned to work from an unpaid vacation in San Francisco (funded by a lucky horse bet at Tanforan Racetrack south of San Francisco), he was offered the chance to transfer to the locally-owned McKesson affiliate in Manila, called Glo-Co. After some thought, he said "yes" and headed for the ship in San Francisco. He was 29.

Naomi arrived in the Bay Area from Philadelphia and boarded the ship, the *S.S. President Harrison*, for Manila. It was mid-1937.

Six weeks can be a long time crossing the Pacific in moonlit tropical waters. In 1928, nearly 10 years earlier, Bob had traveled on the Dollar Lines around the world as crew, playing clarinet and piano in the ship's band with his brother Gilbert and two Azusa friends. He fancied himself something of a world traveler. In 1937, the *President Harrison* was following a similar route to the one Bob had taken in 1928. Bob's cabin-mate—four days out from San Francisco—asked him to "vacate" their tiny second-class cabin for a couple of hours since he was interested in this single traveler, "Miss Bishop." Miss Bishop did not value the attention which immediately piqued Bob's interest. The unsuccessful cabin-mate "pursuit" occupied some of the remaining three days from San Francisco to Honolulu. Leaving Hawaii and Bob's cabin-mate behind, the *Harrison* began the long trans-Pacific journey. Bob offered to be a tour guide for Naomi in the various cities they would be visiting: Yokohama, Shanghai, and Hong Kong. "Just friends," he explained, also touting his "experiences" from 10 years before. She agreed. So, after fully using the local American Express tours her father had paid for, she extended her city visits with Bob—a very different experience.

In Shanghai, Bob took Naomi on a rickshaw ride around part of the city beyond the International Settlement and near the Suzhou River area, "just for the experience." After half an hour, he told the Chinese man pulling the rickshaw to take them to their hotel; he gave the name and address in the International Settlement where the steamship company had provided lodging for travelers while the ship discharged and collected cargo at the harbor. The coolie stopped at a different hotel near the Bund.

"This is not the hotel," Bob said. The coolie looked at him and then at Naomi. "One hotel is as good as another." He smiled, looking at Naomi. There was a short, loud argument, but at the end, with a Chinese crowd forming around them, Bob grudgingly paid the rickshaw man, swallowing hard. It was 1937, the sixth year of the Sino-Japanese war in Manchuria, and Shanghai outside the International Settlement was verging on chaos with the Japanese army pushing through the surrounding outskirts, threatening invasion of the city itself, which they did a few weeks after Bob and Naomi arrived in Manila. It was no time for a dispute on a Shanghai city street. The couple got out of the rickshaw, entered the hotel, and ordered a taxi from the front desk to take them to the correct hotel.

In Manila, Naomi introduced Bob to her brother, 1st Lt. George Bishop, who in turn, over the coming months, introduced Bob to the Army-Navy Club, the Elks Club, the Manila Polo Club and similar Philippine colonial American haunts.

During her visit, Lt. Bishop took his sister to an American-Filipino reception in Manila, where she was fortunate to meet the President of the Philippine Commonwealth, Manuel Quezon. She was dazzled, but still had to sail on again nearly two weeks after she arrived in Manila, continuing her around-the-world voyage home.

When she arrived home in Laurel weeks later, there was a letter waiting from Bob proposing marriage. She accepted by return mail. She had to work almost 18 months, fulfilling her Delaware school contract and putting together the money to return to Manila, which she did in 1939. They were married in July that year.

Colonial Manila

For the months while waiting, Bob and his soon-to-be brother-in-law, George, became quite friendly. Finding out that Bob liked to play bridge and was quite accomplished, Lt. Bishop wrangled invitations for him to join a number of Army-Navy Club bridge tournaments. After the war, George reminded him of one match Bob had subsequently forgotten in Manila in late 1937. One tournament champ was a Maj. Dwight Eisenhower, who went on to other bigger things. Bob hadn't remembered the tournament, coming in some distance behind the leaders. Eisenhower was only a major of no particular note that no one had ever heard of. "Damn good player," Bob said, once reminded of the match.

While waiting, Bob first took a room in Manila's Luneta Hotel, just a few blocks off Dewey Boulevard near Luneta Park, not far from his work. Shortly after, he moved into the University Club Apartments, a seven-story, 44-room hotel-apartment building built in the early 1930s and popular with Americans, just next door to the Luneta Hotel and managed by the hotel. The University Club building was later demolished after the war, but the hotel is still there today. In the bar at the Luneta, he met Frank Foley, a salesman and purchasing manager for a New York hemp and jute trading company, awaiting the arrival in November 1937 of his wife, Ella, and daughter, Mary Alice, from the U.S.; he was also a resident of the University Club. It is hard to tell which man was the better storyteller, but each night in the hotel bar next door before dinner, the two men would soon have a group around them drinking, talking, and laughing. The Foley family and Bob became close as the months passed, particularly enjoying the Manila Polo Club where Bob played baseball for one of the four club league teams, the *"Whites,"* while he awaited the arrival of his bride-to-be.

Things were not going well for the Foley family, however. While Mary Alice was quite happy at Maryknoll Normal School, a Catholic private school in Manila, her mother, Ella, was finding adjustment to Philippine life difficult. The family lived at the University Club, which meant that most household chores were taken care of by the hotel staff from next door. Ella was bored. She spent her time at the Polo Club with the few friends she had made, and in some church affairs or shopping, often going to movies sometimes two or three times a week. Later, in her diary, she would write: "Manila would be a terrible future home."

The economic recession of 1937 hit Frank's firm hard. They were in the import/export business, and it began to fall apart. In July 1938, some months after the recession hit its peak, and after only about a year in the Philippines, the family decided to return to New York. The news there was very bad. Frank's company filed for bankruptcy protection, and Frank found himself unemployed. The only positive was that Frank, suspecting the worst, had made contact before he left Manila with a Philippine company trading in sugar and coconut oil, looking for a trading executive. He got a job offer from them in late 1938 while in New York and returned to Manila in early 1939, followed some months thereafter by his not-so-happy wife and contented daughter. Of course, he contacted Bob Smith, who was still living at the University Club apartments, and their friendship was renewed. When the rest of the Foley family arrived in late 1939, Mary Alice enrolled at the American School in Manila as a freshman.

In June 1939, just weeks before Naomi was scheduled to arrive on the *S.S. President Pierce*, Bob asked Frank to be his best man—"stand up with him," Frank always said.

"You know I would do it, but the church won't let me," the devout Catholic Foley tried to explain to the son of a Baptist minister. Not unusually, the ongoing discussion was lubricated by Cutty Sark Scotch and so became rather convoluted as it proceeded. Eventually, Frank suggested they go see the priest "who can explain it better than I can."

A day or two later, they sat with the priest, who quietly listened as the two friends continued the debate, fortunately minus the Scotch. Finally, he had listened enough and raised his hand: "I think Mr. Foley is old enough and wise enough not to be corrupted by joining his friend in this ceremony." He smiled. The two friends looked at each other and nodded. Clearly, the priest could explain it well.

Ironically, the Protestant minister who officiated at the wedding ceremony at Manila's Union Church on July 10 was also a Foley, one of the preeminent church leaders in the country, and later a leader in the Santo Tomas camp. His name was Dr. Walter Brooks Foley, and he greeted Frank as a fellow "heretic," a relationship the devoutly Catholic Frank quickly sought to disavow. In the families, Dr. Foley was always known as the "holy Foley," and Frank, of course, as the "un-holy Foley."

The wedding took place only some 10 weeks before the German invasion of Poland launched the full force of World War II. At that time, the U.S. government told civilian families in the Philippines "they would be safe," Mary Alice would later recall, "so we stayed."

On the six-week 1939 crossing on the *S.S. President Pierce*, Naomi became close with a fellow passenger, Martha Gray, a Southern woman from North Carolina tobacco country; "we're just little tobacco people," Martha always said. One of her relatives had helped endow the Bowman Gray Medical School at Wake Forest University, so "little tobacco" was a relative term. Naomi had spent many years in both North and South Carolina, where her father had owned a timber business prior to and during World War I so she and Martha had much in common. Martha was quite interested in Anthony M. (Tony) Balkunas, the second officer on the *Pierce,* and vice versa. The three became a "gang" during the slow-boat crossing, visiting sights and enjoying restaurants at ports they visited, with Naomi "acting" chaperone, as was "appropriate." Since Naomi's family were all in the United States—her brother, George, nearly a year earlier having been reassigned stateside by the Army, she asked Tony Balkunas to give her away at the wedding. The *Pierce* was scheduled to be in Manila for several days attending to its cargo business. Relishing the break from his duties on board, Tony was delighted to be part of the wedding. Martha attended the ceremony before continuing on her around-the-world trip. He and Martha were married in North Carolina a year later.

During the war, Tony served in the Navy. Shortly after the liberation of the Philippines, his ship was in and out of Manila twice. He tried to see if the Smiths were still there, but with limited shore leave, he could find out nothing. He didn't tell Martha at the time, fearing the worst. Some five or six years after the war, at dinner in Burlingame across San Francisco Bay from the Smiths, he recounted the story, commenting: "There was so much chaos and destruction, I couldn't find out any information in the short time I had. I was really worried."

Quietly, Naomi added: "I know what you mean. Between liberation and repatriation, I tried to get birth certificates for the boys. I knew I would need them later. It took me hours over several days to find the vital records office, or anyone who knew anything, with virtually no public transport, no cabs, nothing. A mess. The destruction was stunning ... buildings burned, walls shattered from gun fire, rubble still in streets. But the Filipino government people were so kind and helpful that I finally found the right office and the right bureaucrat to get certified copies of both birth certificates. I'm so glad we got those things." Thinking ahead and careful planning were traits Naomi had all her life and served her well during the coming internment.

Infamy

December 8, 1941 (Monday)
Manila

Yesterday—Sunday, December 7—had been a typical mid-winter weekend day in the Philippine capital, partially cloudy with temperatures in the mid-80s. Winter in Manila is one of the best times in that tropical city with humidity at a comfortable level and temperatures ranging from the low 70s at night into the upper 80s in daytime. Weekends were very relaxed for the American colonial elites. In Honolulu, on the other side of the International Date Line, it was still Saturday, December 6, and quiet, except in the bars and dives along Hotel Street.

Naomi and Bob had risen Sunday mid-morning, enjoying the end of a normal weekend. Bob had been brushing his teeth in the bright sunny bathroom while the young teenage house boy was standing quietly barefoot, leaning against the door jamb at the side, watching. Bob set his toothbrush on the sink edge and it slipped and fell off, landing on the polished dark wooden bathroom floor. The house boy reached over with his foot, gripped the toothbrush with his toes, lifted it, and handed it to Bob. He was startled, but took it and put it back on the sink. Later, when the house boy was gone, Bob threw the toothbrush away.

Often on Sunday, Naomi went to church, the same one where she had been married two and a half years earlier, but Bob, a preacher's son, did not, for his own reasons. This early

21

December morning, Naomi decided to stay home from church as well. They planned to have a late breakfast and then go to the Manila Polo Club, where Bob was captain of the *Whites* baseball team, one of four club teams: the *Blues, Reds, Whites,* and *Greens.* His team had won the Club's *Saleeby Trophy* earlier in 1941. In September, Bob and Naomi playing with three other club members as the *Goodriches* team in the Polo Club Mixed Duck Pin Bowling Tournament, had been named runners-up, coming in second. Bob had been team captain as well. Life was good. Even middle-class families had excellent household help, often two or more people.

The Polo Club was *the* gathering place for the American expat community in Manila—dinners, dances, polo of course, drinks on the verandah, all situated right on Manila Bay with exquisite sunset views over the Bay, the American Asiatic Fleet lying at anchor not far off the club beach. The facility was in Pasay City, only a few miles south, along the bay from the apartment Bob and Naomi had in Malate, another Manila barrio. After the war, the club lands would be expropriated by the Philippine government and the club would relocate to its present-day location in Makati City, Metro Manila.

Since no club baseball league games were scheduled with the season over now that it was early December and holiday time, Bob thought he would try to put together a pick-up game. They would have a late lunch afterward and maybe the Foleys would be at the club for lunch too. The Chinese amah, Kong, would take care of the baby, Bobby, who was now over seven months old, and would give him lunch and a nap after he played on the grounds at the Sikia Apartments on Avenue M.H. del Pilar, not far off Dewey Boulevard, which skirted around the shore of Manila Bay. The Smiths had moved there from the University Club a year and a half before. Just a few days earlier, in late November, Naomi had been told by her doctor that her suspicion was correct. She was almost two months along in the pregnancy for her second child. They hoped for a girl this time. She was feeling a little unwell, and so they let the morning drift away and Bob decided to forgo the potential pick-up game. They would go later for lunch at the club. It was a lovely, casual, tranquil, uneventful Sunday, the last they remembered from their years in Manila.

The next morning—Monday, December 8 (December 7 in Honolulu)—was expected to be a slow business day in the capital. It was the Catholic Feast of the Immaculate Conception, one of the most important festivals across this very Catholic country and viewed by many as an unofficial start to the Christmas season. Attendance at Mass started early and continued through the morning. Many of the workers at Glo-Co, Bob's company, were taking the whole day off, so Bob decided he would delay going into work until after lunch.

The first air raids on Greater Manila by the Japanese bombers and fighters came after 11 a.m. local time, focused on army and navy installations. The initial attacks were distant and not particularly understood by the civilians. "What's going on?" some would ask. "Is it a drill?" The military positions were quite far from the apartment on M.H. del Pilar. Then on the radio, the reports started to come in, announcements for soldiers and sailors to report to their units, and news of the attacks. And the world changed forever.

Although there had been military shortwave radio reports to Philippine Army headquarters from Honolulu about the attack on Pearl Harbor as early as 3 a.m. Manila time, bureaucratic bumbling had prevented proper response. It was reported later that aides to Gen. Douglas MacArthur even failed to wake him immediately to tell him of the Honolulu reports. The Japanese attacks on Manila came from Formosa Island, a Japanese-occupied "protectorate" for about a half century some 200 miles north of the Philippines. The attackers were delayed by some six hours from their original schedule, which had been intended to coincide with the Pearl Harbor attack, due to fog and inclement weather on Formosa. Still nearly half of the U.S. B-17 bombers and P-40 pursuit fighters on the Manila air fields were caught on the ground and destroyed. Within a week, the United States Army Air Force (USAAF) had been virtually wiped out, except for a handful of B-17s which escaped to Australia. Attacks on the ships of the U.S. Asiatic Fleet had caused those vessels to depart Manila Bay for pre-planned deployment outside Manila Bay.

As the day progressed, from many places around the city, bombing and smoke could be heard and seen centered on the military installations at Clark and Nichols airfields and Cavite navy base, but no bombs landed near the Smith apartment and the initial sounds were muffled and distant. Reports on civilian radio were vague and contradictory, except the advice to stay indoors and keep off the roads. The Chinese amah Kong seemed to be oblivious to the news reports, simply taking care of Bobby as usual. Naomi later said she believed that Kong didn't pay attention to the radio reports since they were in English, and the Manila attacks were distant. Once, almost a year earlier when Kong first came to them in preparation for Bobby's birth, Naomi had mentioned to her the sad situation, the death and destruction from the war in China reported in the papers and on radio. Kong had looked at her impassively, and then quietly had said: "Little man come ... little man go. China still China." Now no one took the middle-aged Chinese woman aside and explained what was going on, at least in part since no one really knew. Later she seemed to become aware and concerned, but still focused on "my Bobby."

Throughout the day, they sat listening to the radio and then ate a light supper. There was nothing they could do, and so they went to bed. Sleep was fitful, but the sounds of bombing and firing faded in the night, since, unknown to the Manila residents, the planes had returned north to their Formosa bases.

Together

The Chinese amah left early in the morning as she began fully to comprehend the situation.

"Can't stay, missie," Kong said. "The little man is coming, with more bombs. It's okay for you, but I can't stay. I have to leave. I'll come back to see the boy." She had been with them since just before the baby, Bobby, was born seven plus months earlier. He was thriving under her care and attention. Already he stood at the side of the crib, holding on and jumping, laughing and babbling, fat, blond, and blue-eyed.

The first air raid had come in the mid-morning the day before, and since then, there had been attacks on the harbor and airport during the day. Rumors scuttled in and out of the houses and apartments. *They* had been stopped on the beach. *They* were landing in the south. There was bombing near Bagio. The Army was heading north on the military defense highway. Everybody had a story; no one had any facts. There was no business. Life had come to a standstill. The Smith household staff of three had all left the day before.

The Foleys had moved in the spring of 1941 to a lovely house south of the Army Air Base at Nichols Field. Frank called the afternoon of the first raid on Monday.

He was surprised the phone had worked. His wife, Ella, was in a panic. The bombing at the airfield had started again early that Monday morning and was only a few hundred yards from their new home. He was trying desperately to find a room in a hotel in downtown Manila. It should be safer. But nothing was available. Many of the hotels had closed, their staff fleeing or melting back into the local populace and heading into rural Luzon.

Bob insisted the Foleys stay with them in the Sikia Apartments on M.H. del Pilar. It was much farther from the airfield than the Foleys' house and not near navy facilities. Anyway, Kong had left and her room was available. With school closed, the Foleys' teenage daughter, Mary Alice, now some 16 years old, could babysit Bobby. It would be crowded, but the company would be comforting. Frank took him up on the offer at once. But it was three days before they arrived from less than ten miles away.

Mary Alice recalled later: "We lived quite close to the Army Air Base at Nichols Field and the thud of bombs and the shaking of the ground as they fell were incredible.

"My first courageous step into World War II was to put a pillow over my head. We were up, dressed, and out of the house in minutes, and I found myself clutching three things of obviously great value to me: my eyeglasses, silver rosary beads, and a cigar box of money.

"Our house was one of several in a U-shaped compound, and as we reached the entrance, the road in front ... the main road out of Manila ... was choked with Filipinos streaming out of the area. Piled high in two-wheeled pony-drawn carts were household goods, squawking fighting cocks, and elderly grandmothers. The sky to the south was red from the fires set off by the bombs and anti-aircraft guns, but by this time, the planes had all gone and all you could hear was the shuffle of feet and the creak of the cart wheels.

"Tuesday was fairly quiet and we stayed close to home, not knowing what to anticipate. We soon found out. On Wednesday, December 10, as we were preparing to move in with friends in Manila proper (*the Smiths*) further away from the airfield, the air raid sirens blew and we hit the dirt in front of the house as wave after wave of Japanese bomber formations flew over us on their way to bomb the Naval Station at Cavite. Within an hour, Cavite lay in ruins and 1,600 men were dead.

"The road to Manila was impassable, and we headed in the opposite direction to spend the following two nights and days in the car under a tree. The tropical mosquitoes had a feast. We finally reached our friends in Manila on the third day and remained with them."

A New Yorker, Frank had never learned to drive, but his driver, Manuel, stayed with them, driving the car, loaded with clothes, food, and valuables, as they tried to reach the Smiths' apartment. Manuel helped unload. But he wanted to leave.

"Sir," he said. "I will visit my family for a time. But, sir, when the Jap bastards have been thrown into the sea, I will come back." Frank had agreed. He could do little else, and one less mouth to feed was probably good. Manuel parked the Studebaker in the apartment parking lot behind the building, gave Frank the keys, and left.

The Rifle

Sikia Apartments
Mid-December

The two families settled into a routine, the women sharing the cooking and the clean-up. Frank and Bob spent an hour or two at their offices, alone except for one or two people there, trying to find information. They would meet for a drink at the Luneta Hotel around noon time. Mary Alice took the baby for a walk in the park across the street. It was surprisingly placid. The radio talked of the war, but for them, away from the bombing of military facilities, it seemed to be somewhere else. The general bombing had now stopped for a time.

About ten days before Christmas, two soldiers and an Army officer came by the apartment. One soldier was carrying a World War I vintage Enfield rifle. The other had a clipboard with typed papers on it, which he marked up as they went along.

"Army orders are to distribute weapons to American civilians registered with our headquarters for their protection in case anything happens," the lieutenant said.

"What the hell am I going to do with a rifle?" Bob asked. "I don't even know how to shoot one." He looked over at Frank, who shrugged.

"I was in the flying service in the Great War," Frank said. "Never shot a damned thing except in training ... which was thirty years ago."

"Orders," the lieutenant said and handed the rifle to Bob, along with a box of cartridges. He turned and walked down the hall of the apartment, looking at the checklist in his hand. Bob closed the door. He put the rifle on the dining room table, and he and Frank stood staring at it. They decided that Bob's connection with the Army through Naomi's brother George was the likely reason his name was on the list.

"I'll get the Scotch," Frank said finally. He went to the cupboard in the kitchen, took down the Cutty Sark, got two glasses, and came back to the dining room. Bob went back into the kitchen and got a bottle of soda water and a tray of ice. They sat at the dining room table, each sipping his drink.

"What the hell do we do with that?" Bob said after a time. Frank shook his head slowly. By the time the women and Mary Alice came back from the market, the men were on their second drink. They had taken the instruction sheet and disassembled the rifle, removing the cartridge holder and slipping the bolt out. The rifle was new, still carrying its grease protection. It needed cleaning. The box of cartridges sat closed at the side.

"What is that?" Naomi said. "And what's it doing in here?"

"And why is it on the dining room table?" Ella said. The two men explained the visit from the Army.

"Get rid of it," Naomi said.

"Yes. We're going to fix dinner. Get it out of here, Frank," Ella said. The men looked at each other, finished their drinks, and stood up.

"That's just what we should do," Bob said. They picked up the pieces of the rifle and the box of cartridges, each putting on a coat for the cool evening, and left the apartment.

It was only a few blocks from the apartment to the waterfront on Manila Bay.

Dewey Boulevard curved along the lovely bayside, running at an angle to their avenue, M.H. del Pilar. The December air was lovely, cool, and soft, bracing and sobering them as they walked to the bay. Overhead the palm trees whispered in the light breeze. It helped sober them, too.

"Do you think we're doing the right thing?" Bob asked.

Frank paused a moment. "Neither of us knows a damned thing about this rifle. If the Japs come and we've got a gun, it could be a real problem." Bob nodded. Frank hefted the box of cartridges and threw it as far into the bay as he could.

"Boy, that was weak," Bob said. "Step back." He took the rifle by the barrel and swung it around in a circle several times, gaining speed. At the third spin, he flung the rifle into the bay. Frank threw the spring mechanism and bolt as far as he could. They stood by the bay a minute, looking at the ripples where the rifle had disappeared into the water.

"How about another Scotch?" Frank asked.

"Let's do her!" Bob said.

Trucks

Late December, 1941

The Japanese air attacks had started mid-day on December 8, and then returned intermittently but continuously over the following days and then weeks. The American airfields and naval facilities were hard hit. Surprise had been achieved. Martial law was declared by the military and agreed by High Commissioner Sayre and President Quezon.

Soon after the initial bombing, the U.S. Army contacted the Glo-Co Company's general manager and president, Robert Cromwell, Bob's boss, as they did many companies across the city. They needed help. Mr. William Zeitlin, representing Lt. Col. Quinn's office, who was coordinating all transport on the island of Luzon, had been designated by the Army to get trucks from wherever he could to transport troops, supplies, anything. Many army vehicles had been destroyed or damaged in the initial days of the war. Cromwell agreed Glo-Co would help and turned the job over to Bob, who was the secretary and treasurer of the company and would have the records.

Bob went over to the company factory and warehouse. He left Naomi at the apartment with their son. She was nervous at his leaving, but it couldn't be helped. The Foleys were there, which was a relief. She spent the time packing, just to be prepared for she knew not what.

31

Glo-Co made cosmetics such as hair cream, tooth powder and tooth paste, perfumes, soap, as well as aspirin and talcum powder in the Manila factory, which Bob also oversaw because of his education as a graduate chemist. The company also distributed pharmaceuticals mostly imported from McKesson in Los Angeles. They had a fleet of seventeen trucks, quite new, mostly Fords, many from 1940 and 1941 model years; three-quarter ton, one ton, and one-and-a-half ton panel delivery vehicles. Before the war, the company had employed about 250 people throughout the Philippines.

Bob understood that the company would need some vehicles for their own purposes—moving inventory, supplies or equipment as much out of danger as they could—so he asked the Army to leave them some vehicles for a time. Zeitlin agreed to take twelve trucks, mostly the newest ones, for now. Bob talked with Jesus Leonidez, one of his key managers, and Joseph Saint Theresa, his assistant. They tried to line up some drivers, but with all the confusion from the war, they could only find two. The army didn't care. They filled in with their own troopers as well. Two additional trucks in Cebu and three in Mindanao were handed over, all coordinated between Bob and Zeitlin over Army signal corps telephone. The seven trucks in Manila were driven to the U.S. Armed Forces Motor Pool Headquarters in Manila in a couple of batches. The Army also commandeered from the company inventory some 430 flashlights and 800 cases of soap.

There was no paperwork, just verbal instructions and a verbal agreement that the Army would compensate the company "at a later date." Cromwell, the primary owner of Glo-Co, spent nearly five years after the war assisted by Bob getting compensation, by which time the company had ceased to function.

Bob asked Jesus to drive one of the trucks the company was retaining for a couple of weeks to the apartment where Bob lived. It was an insurance policy in case the Smiths needed to move trunks, furniture, or other heavy bulky things "somewhere safe." The truck was left parked behind the apartment.

Bob was gone over three hours, during which time there were additional raids by the Japanese, although not particularly close to the apartment. Naomi was very worried, mostly about her baby, but also about Bob. Still, she held herself on a tight leash. Once they were back together, seemingly like a miracle, the raids tailed off and then stopped. They did not know where the raids came from and that it was likely the distance between Formosa and Manila that dictated the attack cycle.

Lingayen

On December 22, 1941, the main Japanese Army landed at Lingayen Gulf, some 120 miles north of Manila. The Philippine Commonwealth Army outnumbered the Japanese by nearly three to one, but they were mostly raw recruits, the embryo of an army planned to be in service in 1946, the date the U.S. had set for independence for the islands in a law passed in 1934. These soldiers were no match for the highly trained Japanese troops, many of whom had fought in China for years earlier.

Defensive lines set up north of Manila fell readily to the invaders. At Christmas Eve, MacArthur withdrew his forces from Manila to Corregidor and Bataan, declaring the capital an "open city."

The Japanese took control, arriving in Manila on January 2. Shortly thereafter, the local civilian population was rounded up.

The Chest

Manila
Pre-Christmas, December, 1941

When MacArthur declared Manila an open city at Christmas, and especially for those paying attention, it was clear that the Japanese would be occupying the city within days. The four adults, the Smiths and the Foleys, sat around the dining room table. Across from them in the living room, two steamer trunks and three suitcases stood open. Clearly, they would not hold much. Mary Alice, a young teen, holding Bobby, sat quietly across the room on the sofa.

"We've got the truck from the plant out back," Bob said. "We can haul the trunks to the warehouse."

"Will it be safe?" Naomi asked.

"I don't know ... maybe ... but maybe not. Anyway, leaving the things here will not be an option. I suspect these apartments will be turned over to the Japs, for officers or whatever. Anything we leave we will likely never see again."

Frank looked up at Bob and then over at Ella. "I guess our stuff is out of the question," he asked. Ella nodded.

"We could use the car to go get some things." She paused. "But they're just things we can replace anyway."

"Except the pictures." It was Mary Alice, Bobby in her lap, seated on the couch in the small living room talking across the open trunks. They looked at each other, but knew there was nothing to do.

"We brought some of those with us," Ella said. "They'll just have to do."

"I don't think it's smart to go back toward the airfield anyway," Bob said. Frank nodded.

"It's one of the first places the Japs will go," Frank said. "Besides, Ella is right; it's just stuff."

Carefully, Naomi sorted through the apartment closets and dressers, through the kitchen and pantry. Slowly, the steamer trucks filled up. They reserved what they might need over the next few days, packing those in the smaller suitcases. Ella and Mary Alice put some of their excess things in one trunk. But no one knew how long they might need to plan for. Or what they would need. There had been no information you could rely on—just rumors and "chatter" as Naomi liked to call it. *Where would you go, for how long, and what could you get later? Could you come home after? After what?*

Several hours later, the trunks and cases were full, overfull, in fact. "Look at all the stuff we still have left. And there's no room," Naomi said. She began to unpack one of the trunks, sorting again what would be taken and what left. Ella had been bent over a suitcase packing. As she straightened up, she looked across the room under the large main window.

"What about the chest?" She pointed at a carved Chinese camphor chest, one of the first things Naomi had bought after coming to Manila two years before. Her brothers had sent her money as a wedding present, and she had used it for the chest. She had it packed with special linens, a Philippine banana-cloth table set and other special items, photos, and silver.

"Bob," she called. "Can we take the camphor chest, too?"

"Sure, why not?"

Naomi and Ella opened the chest and removed its contents, spreading them on the floor, sofa and chairs. Slowly, Naomi walked around, looking at the things spread there, then put them in the camphor chest to protect them from insects. She looked around the room, seeing what she was forgetting for the first time.

"I think I'll put the silver cups in the chest," she said. Bob had played baseball, and they had bowled at the Army-Navy Club,

Elks Club, and the Manila Polo Club before the war. They had won nine different cups for the various team victories over the two years. The cups were wrapped and placed in the bottom of the chest. She took her sterling silver flatware out of its chest and wrapped the knives, spoons, and forks in various linens, stuffing them around the sides of the chest. She put their photo album in and all the papers from the wedding. Two paintings they had bought on their honeymoon and some Chinese art Naomi had bought also were carefully wrapped and laid in. On top, she put the banana-cloth table set and her evening gowns. The chest was full.

The next day, the Glo-Co staff members Jesus and Joseph came to help with the truck. They hoisted the steamer trunks into the back part of the truck bed and then the camphor chest. The suitcases were kept in the apartment. Bob and Frank crowded into the front with Joseph driving, and Jesus bounced along in the back with the trunks.

At the Glo-Co warehouse, everything was unloaded. Using a dolly, they wedged the steamer trunks into a corner. But the camphor chest was considered too fragile to use the dolly, so two other warehouse workers who happened to be there helped carry it upstairs into the file storage area where the office workers kept the company's old papers. They pushed the chest into a corner. A minute later, Frank came up the stairs carrying an old, stained canvas sheet.

"Let's wrap this around it to keep the crap off," he said. They did and then pushed the wrapped chest back in amongst the file cabinets, cases, and cardboard boxes.

A few days later, the U.S. Army collected the Glo-Co truck Bob had been using for transport of the steamer trunks. It was driven off toward Bataan and was never heard from again.

Days after liberation, over three years later, Bob returned to the Glo-Co warehouse. It had been damaged by the liberation fighting and the downstairs factory area had been cleaned out, the offices too, sometime during occupation. The steamer trunks were gone, as well as the pill-making machinery, packaging and packing equipment, desks, typewriters, phones—everything.

The warehouse was a dirty, empty room with broken windows on one side. But overhead, up in the file storage area, seemingly nothing had been touched. He could see the dirty canvas-wrapped chest, papers and trash on top, sitting just where they had put it, wood and metal file cabinets around it. Later, with the help of the U.S. Navy, the chest was consigned to a vessel heading home to San Francisco. It arrived months later than planned. During the voyage, the left rear foot of the chest was damaged by rats gnawing at it. It was the only damage the chest suffered in the war. All the contents, the important "stuff" from before the war, were intact.

The Car

Frank Foley was a successful businessman. He had lived in Manila twice for nearly four years. He owned a 1934 Studebaker President, a large four-door, gray-green sedan. His driver's name was Manuel, and pre-war, Frank would sit in the back of the car reading the *Manila Times* on his way to his office. The colonial life suited him, and he was content. Once, to Frank's amusement, Manuel had remarked, speaking over his shoulder to Frank in the back: "Sir, when independence comes, then things will be different." In the Philippine Independence Act passed by Congress in 1934, a phased process of independence was established ending on July 4, 1946 with a free Philippine Republic. Already as an early step, in 1935, a president of the Philippine Commonwealth had been elected, Manuel Quezon.

"Oh? How?" Frank had asked, putting down his newspaper to listen.

"With independence, I will sit in the back of the car and you will drive." Manuel turned and smiled at Frank. Frank smiled back. "Just drive and watch the damn road." He resumed reading his paper.

Of course, no such thing could occur due to the simple fact that Frank did not know how to drive. He was born in New York City, in Queens, in the late 1890s. He attended school in the city and graduated from the ninth grade at PS116, ending his formal attendance in the New York Public School System. He took a job as a runner at the mercantile exchange and began learning what was necessary to buy and sell things you did not own. His friend Bob once said, "Frank Foley can sell anything he can touch. But if he can't see it, he can't sell it." He learned much at the exchange, but he did not learn how to drive. What need was there in New York City?

When the Foleys moved in with the Smiths after the bombing began at the airfield, his driver, Manuel, parked Frank's Studebaker in the rear of the apartment building and gave him the keys, leaving Manila and returning to his family in the north of Luzon. When anyone needed to go anywhere in those tense times, Bob or Naomi drove in their 1935 Buick. They called it the "Termite Hotel" because its wooden frame had been infested with termites two years earlier and had had to be rebuilt. The arrangement worked just fine for Frank.

The Japanese took control in Manila on January 2. They were organized and efficient people, examining the records in the Manila city offices and the Philippine Commonwealth Government offices. Of particular interest were vehicles, and small squads of soldiers were sent to the addresses listed in the government records to collect the various cars and trucks. A squad of three soldiers and a second lieutenant arrived at the Sikia Apartments. They knocked on the door of the Smith apartment.

The lieutenant had a little English. He showed Bob the typed sheet from the motor vehicle office.

"Where is car?"

"In the back," Bob said.

"Show." Bob led the lieutenant and the three soldiers down the stairs and around to the back where the Buick was parked.

"Keys." Bob handed them over.

"Now start." Bob got in and started the Buick. "Out," the lieutenant said, and one of the soldiers climbed in behind the wheel and ground the transmission into gear, lurching out the back of the apartment and onto M.H. del Pilar. Bob never saw the car again.

"Whose car?" the lieutenant said, pointing at the Studebaker.

"Mr. Foley. He's staying with us. And his family, too."

With the two remaining soldiers, the lieutenant led the way back up to the apartment. Frank was standing in the kitchen.

"Take car," the lieutenant said.

"What?"

"Take car." His voice rose slightly as he suspected resistance from Frank.

"Give him the damn car," Bob said softly. Frank looked around at the men, two soldiers with rifles, bayonets fixed, and the short, mad lieutenant.

"I'll get the keys." One of the soldiers followed him to his room and stayed close as he returned. The squad made their way down to the rear of the apartment.

"Start car."

Frank took out the keys and looked around, then slid into the driver seat. He put the key in the ignition and turned it. Nothing happened. He felt sweat on his forehead.

"Start car." The lieutenant was mad, now sure he was being made a fool of by the American. Frank shrugged.

"I don't know how to drive."

The lieutenant un-snapped the cover on his pistol. "I don't know how," Frank said. Slowly the Japanese drew his pistol.

"Let me try," Bob said. Frank slid out of the driver seat, and Bob climbed in behind. He had never driven a Studebaker. He glanced around the dash board and saw nothing.

"Start car!"

Bob felt around with his foot. Nothing. He bent down to look and saw nothing. He slid further up in the seat and felt higher up the firewall with his foot and hit something. He pressed down and the car lurched forward, the four men outside jumping out of the way. Bob put the clutch in and pressed the starter again, and the Studebaker came to life.

"Get out." Bob put the car in neutral and pulled on the parking brake, and another soldier climbed in behind the wheel. He was a better driver than the first and took the car smoothly out of the parking lot and onto the street.

The lieutenant put his pistol back in his holster, glared at Frank, and led his other remaining soldier away.

"Shit," Frank said.

"I didn't know you couldn't drive."

"Well, I never needed to before," Frank said.

"Would have helped today."

Santo Tomas

Manila
January, 1942

Santo Tomas University is a Catholic school (the Pontifical and Royal University of Saint Thomas), one of the oldest existing in Asia and one of the oldest in the world, having been founded in 1611 by the Spanish Dominicans. It is still a busy, functioning first-rate institution of higher learning today.

In early1941, a group of American business and city leaders in Manila became concerned as war swirled across Europe and China. Approaches were made to the American High Commissioner in Manila, Francis B. Sayre. "Perhaps women and children should be repatriated to the United States just as a matter of caution?" But the Roosevelt Administration and the political appointees in Manila were fearful of what a wholesale American evacuation of the islands would mean, absent actual war. Would panic ensue? The American people had jobs, homes, lives in the Philippines. How could that all be uprooted in a state of maybe "mere" alarm? Besides, Sayre, a son-in-law of former President Woodrow Wilson, was only a figurehead, not a decision-maker; he was the "representative of the President of the United States" in Manila, with no executive authority. There was nothing he could do.

In the 1934 Congressional Act setting up the process leading to independence for the Commonwealth, the elected President of the Philippine Commonwealth, Manuel Quezon, was established as the legal executive authority in the island nation. And no one would talk to President Quezon about evacuation or even the internment of Americans. Soothing words mixed with long stretches of silence replaced action, and only a few families packed up and left. Quietly, however, some military officers began suggesting the repatriation of Army and Navy dependents in mid-1941, leaving the civilians to their own devices. The transfer out of Manila for military wives and children went unnoticed generally by civilians since revolving-door transfers were common in the military. Some military families stayed in Manila and were ultimately interned with the civilians in Santo Tomas. Later, the Army nurses were evacuated from the hospitals on Corregidor and Bataan after Gen. Wainwright surrendered to the Japanese. Instead of being sent with the Army troops to POW camps, they were interned with the civilians in Santo Tomas, becoming the only military in the camp.

What the government did not tell the American civilians was that the State Department had decided that any steps to evacuate the American civilians might seriously damage the morale of the Filipino people. So, in the reported words of U.S. Secretary of State Cordell Hull, the American civilians were ultimately "… pawns of war." Whether Secretary Hull ever actually uttered the words "pawns of war," they in fact encapsulated American policy. In the 1948 Congressional hearings on the War Claims Act, it was noted that American civilians living in Europe and Asia before the U.S. entered the war were warned "several times" to leave Europe or Asia with war approaching. But American civilians living in the Philippines were "not warned" by any one at any time.

High Commissioner Sayre and his staff stayed in Manila as well, reasonably confident they would be looked after should worse come to worse. Above it all, however, Gen. Douglas MacArthur remained in his penthouse apartment at the top of the Manila Hotel, his wife Jean and son Arthur with him there. If *he* stayed, what was the worry?

Despite the "official" silence, these same Manila business leaders who had been asking about repatriation decided to form a committee, the American Emergency Committee, to put together plans should the worst happen and the Japanese invade the Philippines. The key question was where all the non-Filipino people might be interned if invasion came and the Philippine Commonwealth Army was defeated. Several locations were identified and scouted out. The University of Santo Tomas was high on the list, as was the Polo Club, and even the old walled city of Intramuros. The committee met with Catholic and university officials to discuss the university option. An agreement was reached between them informally that if the worst came to pass, the university could be made available.

The "emergency" committee put together a report to the high commissioner. It was filed in his office without comment. When the Japanese did invade and were victorious, the report was handed over to the Imperial Japanese Command, who ultimately adopted it as their internment plan.

None of the "non-pawns," the very top civilian officials, American and Filipino, were interned in Manila. Instead, they were evacuated shortly after General MacArthur declared Manila an open city, leaving on Christmas Eve. President Quezon, his family, and key government office holders—as well as High Commissioner Sayre with family and staff—followed MacArthur to Corregidor, leaving Manila on December 24. Having just been re-elected Commonwealth President in November 1941, Manuel Quezon was sworn in for his second term inside the Malinta Tunnel on Corregidor, with periodic enemy shelling adding to the event. Some days later, these civilians were transferred by the Army to Australia and then were repatriated to the United States. Virtually none of the American internees in Manila knew of the evacuation of the key officials to Australia. Throughout the war, President Quezon worked with American politicians in the U.S. helping with propaganda and other measures to support the war effort. President Quezon died in the U.S. in 1944 and was buried in Arlington Cemetery in Washington. After the war, his remains were repatriated to the Philippines, where he was interred in the Manila barrio of Quezon City.

The interest of the Japanese in Santo Tomas in January 1942 revolved around the physical structure of the University. The

Dominicans bought land in 1927 to move the campus to its current site in Sampaloc from Intramuros, Manila's old walled city where the original university had been situated in 1611. A series of modern multi-story concrete buildings—all with water service, sewage, electrical service, lighting, including a school of education, an administration building, a hospital, an annex campus structure, and others—were built after 1927 on about 220,000 square meters, about 55 acres, in what would become in the 14 years before the start of the war a teaming Manila neighborhood.

Of particular note to the Japanese was the fact that the campus was walled about on three sides with masonry walls over 10 feet high. The front of the campus on Espana Street was closed off from the passing traffic by a high fence of vertical steel bars with high gates, and the buildings set far back across open ground from the street. The controlled access made it a perfect place to house nearly 3,700 Allied and suspicious neutral civilians present in Manila when the Japanese took over the city. There was even open land, athletic fields, and such, which might be used by the internees to grow food if needed. Men and women were housed in different buildings and families allowed to construct bamboo and palm frond shanties on the grounds and close to the buildings where they could spend the often steamy hot days together outside the crowded, uncomfortable buildings.

University of Santo Tomas

Manila, Philippines

Early 1940s

Dapitan Avenue

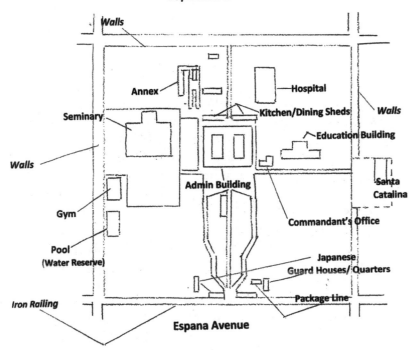

University Life

Manila
Early 1942

The Japanese Army controlled the camp. The internees ran it. In a sense, from the Japanese point of view, these civilian prisoners were a nuisance. The Bushido creed and culture, which was paramount in Japan then, was authoritarian and based on specific roles and behaviors for individuals in society. The Imperial Army was brutal and harsh with Allied soldiers and sailors who had surrendered, an act that in their view was impossible to justify no matter what the circumstances. The consequence of that belief was the infamous Bataan Death March after the American surrender, in which hundreds of American and thousands of Filipino troops died. But the Manila civilians, the women and children and the non-combatant men, were something different, something just inconvenient. It is not clear that the Japanese had any definite idea or plan for dealing with them. They were to be picked up around the city and taken to Santo Tomas in early January. The Japanese had made radio broadcasts and then sent trucks with loudspeakers on them into the city neighborhoods, providing instruction on what was coming. Trucks would come by and the non-Filipino civilians would be picked up, bringing only one suitcase, mosquito netting, and a blanket with them. In other cases, the civilians were ordered to a central location, a ball field or sports venue, where they were picked up. The destination of all was Santo Tomas University.

Both the Smiths and the Foleys were rounded up. But then, a couple of days after being taken to Santo Tomas, Naomi and the baby (and other mothers with children) were told to return home. An internee committee had been set up and decided, with Japanese Army consent, to release some of the prisoners from the camp, which was very overcrowded and unorganized at this early stage. Several release categories were identified and approved by the Japanese, including one for mothers with children under one year of age. Bobby was a little older than eight months at the time.

After this release, Naomi stayed at their apartment for nearly six weeks, able only to communicate with Bob in the camp by the few friends not interned, or short notes passed through the camp gate. It was very stressful for her, worrying about Bob in the camp, trying to find food, and taking care of an active young baby just crawling and getting in trouble, alone and fearful. Streets were patrolled by the Japanese often in small marching squads. Trucks drove past with soldiers riding in the back, their rifles with fixed bayonets clearly visible, the soldiers impassively staring at the people in the streets. There were virtually no Westerners in sight, and the normally outgoing Filipinos were subdued and fearful. Travel by local city bus was intermittent. No other transport was available. Their car was gone, seized by the Japanese. Naomi never wanted to say much about it after the war except once to remark: "It was the worst six weeks of my life."

In mid-January 1942, the Japanese Imperial Army converted the Catholic Holy Ghost College into a "home" for mothers with young children and for sick or orphaned children. Naomi and her baby went there in February, staying until after her second child was born in July. The Holy Ghost Home was not far from Santo Tomas, and she could see Bob almost daily while she was there. Besides, it was "organized," and she was with other mothers as well.

Some months later, when Bob was on an authorized pharmaceutical shopping trip out of the camp, he returned to their apartment. Everything they had left there was gone. Furniture, clothes, pots and pans, dishes, pictures, everything not taken to the Glo-Co warehouse ... all had been removed. By whom and to where, they never found out. All they had is what they had packed and taken with them or stored at the warehouse. He returned to Santo Tomas.

Early in 1942, Naomi, being a school teacher and wanting to have a record of what was happening to give her children later, began a chronology in a child's school notebook, written in pencil in her careful teacher's hand. In it, she recorded that the first internees arrived in Santo Tomas on January 4, 1942. On January 17, the Holy Ghost Home was opened and she went there on February 19 from the apartment with her son Bobby. She was able to travel from Holy Ghost to Santo Tomas daily to eat with Bob and the Foleys from the central camp kitchen and to take care of normal home duties. Finally, on December 29, 1942, having given birth to her second son five months earlier, she returned to Santo Tomas from Holy Ghost with the two children to join Bob, but living apart from him with other mothers and children in the annex inside the internment camp. They spent most days together at their shanty when Bob was not working.

Processes in the camp administration evolved. A committee of internees was set up since no cadre of pre-war Filipino or American officials was present in the camp. The Japanese camp commandant and his staff set harsh rules for behavior, but general in design and limits. For instance, sex by internees was against the rules and could result in severe beating. It didn't stop the sex ... only starvation finally slowed that. In fact, some 45 children were born in 1942 in the camp, dropping to 14 in 1943, the same in 1944, and only two in 1945, as cited by Frederic Stevens in his 1945 book *Santo Tomas Internment Camp*. The big issue, attempted escape, was punishable by death.

Escape was surely out of the question if one thought about it. Luzon Island was thousands of miles of empty ocean behind any fighting front. Americans and European nationals stood out among the Filipino population. To hide, you needed to be in the hills, and they were miles away from Manila, across land occupied by Japanese troops. Escapees would also need some kind of infrastructure in the provinces where they could get support, food, shelter, and help. Many westerners in Manila barely knew people in the local city population well enough to get them to accept such a risk to themselves and their families, let alone strangers in the hinterlands.

Shortly after internment, on the night of February 11, 1942, three internees, two Englishmen, and one Australian climbed over the camp wall and disappeared into the city. Within eight hours, they had been caught by the Japanese. They were returned to the camp, where they were tried by the Japanese for escape, found guilty, and condemned to death. A grave was dug. The men were made to sit on its edge, blindfolded, and shot. The camp internee executive committee was made to watch. Naomi records the event in her notebook chronology, but in a kind of short hand in case the Japanese ever found the notebook. It said simply: "Feb. 15 … Three men." She explained the cryptic note many years after the war.

Executions were rare—ten were recorded in the camp during the whole 37-month internment—but death was not. One man, distraught at the months of internment, threw himself off the roof of the administration building, committing suicide. Of the approximately 3,700 internees, some 390 died between January 1942 and March 1945. Heart failure was the number one cause of death (61), remembering the fairly old age demographic of internees, and malnourishment (55) number two. General geriatric disease was also a common cause of death. Toward the end of her chronology, dated January 31, 1945, Naomi wrote: "Chairman of camp medical staff jailed by Japanese for refusal to exclude the words 'malnutrition' and 'starvation' from death certificates."

The specifics of managing the camp were left by the Japanese to the internee committee and then the sub-committees responsible for various necessary activities, with final say by the Japanese Army, of course. Obvious needs were met: food, sanitation, medical care, and general administration (who was with whom and where, who slept where, and who did what work). As the war continued across the globe, a mail service for prisoners was set up by humanitarian organizations across the war fronts, including the Philippines. Called "Prisoners of War Post ... Service des Prisonniers de Guerre ..." it offered a way to write home. Initially a simple "approved" post card, maximum 25 words, was used, and then letters evolved: one page printed or better typed, one side only. Letters were examined by Japanese and Allied censors, stamped, and dated before being passed through to the recipients. The icing on the cake? They were postage free!

Naomi's letter home dated September 8, 1943 was one of the first she was able to send, beyond the 25-word post cards. It was postmarked September 23, indicating the pace of review and approval, and received at Christmas at her parents' home in Delaware. Her picture of the camp, no doubt presented in the best light to keep her folks from extra worry and to pass the censors, is revealing about life in internment.

She wrote: "The grounds here are like any college campus with many trees for shade. The buildings are of concrete. It is like a small town, for we have schools, churches, markets, a restaurant, sports activities of all kinds, and many vendor stalls where we can buy almost anything. We have our own nipa shack where I take the children all day, and where I can cook extra food over a charcoal stove." (*Nipa is an Asian species of palm tree with feathery leaves used in thatching, and combined with bamboo, to build small one-room shanties.*)

She continued: "The food for us is adequate and nourishing, and for the children it is splendid. They get eggs, milk, fresh vegetables, and fruit every day, and all are thriving. We get bread, fruit, eggs, and vegetables at the market to supplement our meals whenever we want.

"Bob is well and busy. He helps me with the washing and other necessary things for the children, and in addition, works five hours a day in the Hospital Dispensary. He also plays softball in the early evening. I am fine and keep busy all day doing things for the children. Bob and I weigh about the same as when you saw us." Her parents had never met or seen Bob, except in photos.

"We are all well. Bobby is over two years old now. He is very blond and quite fat, and everybody in camp knows him. He roams over practically all of the 54 acres, attends all the softball games in the late afternoon after supper, and goes almost crazy when music is broadcast over the loudspeaker system every evening. He talks incessantly and nearly every day surprises us with some new word in his vocabulary. He also loves to sit on the grinder where rice and corn are ground, and visits the men operating that machine every morning after breakfast. Billy was born in July and is now 14 months old. He has brown hair and brown eyes, and everyone thinks he looks more like Bob than Bobby does. He is beginning to walk now. I had the same doctor and was in the same hospital with him as with Bobby."

She asked her folks to write Bob's mother in Los Angeles and "let her know that we are well."

Naomi's father, George, received the letter on Christmas Eve, 1943, and wrote in reply that same day. It was dated and postmarked December 24. The news was general, but the important information was not included. He did not tell his daughter that her youngest brother, U.S. Army Air Force pilot and Lieutenant Bill Bishop, was missing in action in North Africa. What would be the point?

Mary Alice Foley had a somewhat less positive view of the facilities, especially since she was back in America after the war, remembering life in the camp, not writing a letter to pass through the hands of censors at the time of internment. She recalled: "People were jammed into rooms on cots, if one was available, on bare steel springs, or simply on the floor. Sleeping quarters for men and women were separate. Mom and I were in a room with 40 other women. It had a curtain across the entrance in place of a door and when the wind blew, it raised the curtain horizontally and took the visual protection from the busy hallway with it. After a while this ceased to matter.

"There were three shower heads and four toilet stalls on our floor for several hundred women. Privacy is a casualty of war, and ours was non-existent from day one. You showered companionably with three or four others under one stream of cold water; you were allotted three squares of toilet paper by the assigned bathroom monitor; you stood on line for the four doorless stalls. And you lived with the dictum: 'If you want privacy, close your eyes.'"

She continued: "How did we spend our days? A good portion of the time was spent waiting in line: lines to shower, lines to brush your teeth, food lines, lines to wash your tin cup and plate, lines to do laundry. There were rooms, hallways, and bathrooms to be mopped, and the necessity to carry your cot and bedding out into the sun in an effort to dislodge and squash the carnivorous bedbugs. This was a particularly frustrating job because they always came back.

"In addition to these personal chores, everyone had a community work assignment. These could, and did, range from making soap, carpentry, plumbing, picking worms out of the rice, collecting and burning garbage, working in the kitchen, the hospital, nursing, teaching, soldering tin utensils, and any one of a dozen different jobs required by a community of several thousand."

Mary Alice had several jobs, including later at the age of 18 teaching a class of 46 fifth graders, and from that "deciding I never wanted to be a teacher." She also worked as an aide in the Isolation Hospital, helping the Army nurses who had served at Bataan and Corregidor. She remembered: "They were terrific ... terrifying to those selfishly goldbricking in the early days in an effort to get out of work assignments or to obtain hospital food ... but kind and compassionate to the truly sick and dying. They never stopped going ... never stopped caring."

The Clink

Late 1942

Human beings are an ironic mix—in one sense, adaptive, but also creatures of habit. Several thousand individuals from multiple countries and backgrounds, a wide range of ages, nationality, wealth, position, and experience had been rounded up across Manila and herded together into a 55-acre university campus. Over time, the internee committee, bulwarked by the power and force of the Imperial Japanese Army, had sorted out the mob, assigning living spaces, social infrastructure, schools, food service, as well as trade and commerce with the Filipinos outside the camp. Some called the camp the "clink," slang for jail, or "STIC," short for Santo Tomas Internment Camp. But slowly, all settled into their assigned places. Life must go on.

The expat community in Manila was fairly small and many internees knew others, particularly of the same nationality. The city of Manila had a population estimated in 1939 of about 623,000, with a metro area of about one million plus, with only a tiny percentage non-Filipino. (*By comparison, in 2015 the population of Manila city was 1.78 million and the metro Manila area about 12.8 million. The Philippine nation had a population in 1941 estimated at 17 million, growing to over 100 million by 2015.*) The expats had all gone to the same clubs and attended the same athletic contests, softball or baseball, golf, cricket, and of course, polo. Now, early in the war and the internment, a kind of order had been established. Food was available in the camp and for those with means could be augmented from the outside, as long as the Filipinos had sufficient supply and the Japanese had not yet begun wholesale confiscation of the "surpluses." The Smiths were fortunate since they had support from some of the former Glo-Co employees who came by the camp from time to time. Also, Bob could draw on the company's financial contacts, which he had before the war as treasurer of the company, responsible for a good deal of its banking activities. Neutrals, Swiss, Spanish, and Swedish primarily continued their pre-war activities on a much reduced scale, of course. Bob was able to sign loan documents to be settled after the war with those neutrals to secure cash. From time to time, he would do so and send part of the money on to his former boss, Robert Cromwell, who was interned in the not-too-distant camp of Los Banos. The money was a godsend for both men. As always in life, with money, you can stave off all manner of ill, particularly starvation. As the internment stretched out, Cromwell asked for more money, since the food situation was more dire in Los Banos.

With life after a time settling into a new normal, activities not even dreamed of in the first days of internment were once again mentioned. The students in school put on shows. Games were organized to keep the children occupied, such as play and poetry readings, college quiz teams, boxing matches (particularly for the younger boys), and "endless bridge games." Mary Alice once said: "If incarceration is anywhere in your future, remember that a deck of cards is second only to a toothbrush in order of importance." Naomi records that the first movie was shown in the camp on December 23, 1942. And some of the younger men thought about sports, which many had played pre-war, especially as the cool winter weather arrived.

The Americans got together and decided to play some softball (some reports said baseball). Not all the university's open athletic fields had been plowed over by the internees to grow crops yet. The players had some pickup games, and then the idea of a league of teams to play for a championship was floated. Immediately they did the work to set it up.

They called it the "Clink League." What better title for a group of teams made up of ballplayers incarcerated in an internment camp than a league with teams named for American prisons? There were six teams: "Sing-Sing," "Joliet," "Alcatraz," "Leavenworth," "Atlanta," and "San Quentin." Bob was named acting captain of the Alcatraz team with 13 members. Some of the other teams had one or two more players than Bob's team, but no one cared. The first scheduled game, between Sing-Sing and Joliet, had overflowing attendance, with even some Japanese soldiers looking on, possibly familiar with American softball from pre-war experiences in the United States, or possibly amused and slightly bewildered by American behavior. The name of the winner is lost in time. Bob's team, "Alcatraz," played against "Leavenworth" as the second game scheduled. Bob recalled they lost, but Naomi remembered they won. Over the next weeks, some 15 contests, rotating among the teams, were played.

As spring arrived and the weather became fiercely hot as the tropics often are, the league went on hiatus. Then later, in early 1943, food production became more worrisome and internees began to receive a declining supply. Ball fields were plowed under. The efforts of the internees turned to raising more food rather than athletic contests. Slow starvation reduced energy and desire, and the league never resumed.

The Lab

Santo Tomas
August 1942

The Japanese had no intention of managing the camp—controlling it, yes, but not doing the day-to-day running of the camp. The guards quizzed the internees when they first came in Santo Tomas. "Who is your leader?" The name Earl Carroll was mentioned, and he was tasked by the Imperial Army with appointing hall monitors and other people to help organize the camp. With all the people involved, soon the Internee Committee became too large and unwieldy to manage the camp. An Executive Committee was established from the larger group. It organized and managed the camp until the Japanese Army eventually took over full operation in February 1944 after Allied Forces began to overrun the Japanese Pacific bastions they had gained by their first victories in 1941-1942, closing in on the Philippines and eventually Japan itself, tightening the noose.

Within weeks of opening, the camp grew to several thousand persons, mostly Americans but with large British, Commonwealth and other Allied country contingents, topping out over 5,000. It was so crowded that a satellite camp at Los Banos was opened and Santo Tomas stabilized at about 3,500-4,000 internees. Some "undependable" neutrals also found themselves interned. Organization became paramount, with volunteerism the first method tried. Of course, that was found to be ineffective. Unpleasant jobs—sanitation and the like—began not to be done, and it was found that many skills were present in the camp being used in the wrong places, and soon jobs were being assigned and people were required to perform certain tasks. No work meant no food. It was effective, but not popular always.

Frank was a sales executive and Ella a housewife—not notably helpful in a camp. They were soon assigned jobs, Frank in the kitchen and Ella assisting at school. Mary Alice as a teen was first enrolled in school with the rest of the kids. Naomi had a two-year-old child and another just born, and she was left to take care of them. Bob, as an executive in a pharmaceutical company and a graduate chemist, was ultimately assigned to the camp hospital and dispensary, and a laboratory was set up where various compounds and materials needed for treating the sick could be made or refined. Disinfectant was one continuing need, and a distilling system was set up in the lab using readily available materials to distill alcohol. It was a simple enough process and, when handled "correctly," generated not only the alcohol needed for medical purposes but, in small imperceptible quantities, a proper recreational alcohol for private use. Later, he was assigned to teach chemistry in the school. Mary Alice was one of his students. "I never understood a damned thing about it ... still don't ... but the teacher was 'understanding' ..." she recalled.

One afternoon, an internee unknown to Bob came by the lab. He was wearing one of the camp Executive Committee armbands identifying him as a member. He looked around carefully and then, speaking in a low voice said, "Smitty. We need your help." He looked around again and then reached into his pocket, producing a radio rectifier and two other tubes. "There's a radio that can be of real importance at the right time. When our boys arrive, they will most likely broadcast information we will need. We are hiding parts in various places around the camp where they won't be found. Can you put this someplace?"

"I don't know," Bob said, pausing. "Who are you?"

Still speaking softly, the man said, "That's the point. A few people are asking a few people to hide a few parts. If the Japs find out, no one knows who gave what to whom. Couldn't tell them anything even if tortured. That way, we can protect the radio and the people who are helping. I don't need to tell you my name. It is of no importance."

Bob thought for a minute. He was reluctant, with a wife and children in the camp. Outside in the hallway, there was the sound of someone walking. The man thrust the three parts at Bob, who took them while turning to look at the lab door. Outside, someone unseen passed. When Bob turned back, the man was moving toward the door, not even looking back.

Glancing around the lab, Bob decided to put the radio parts into several of the large glass jars of bulk chemicals carefully lined up in plain sight on the shelving in the lab. Some jars were made of colored glass to filter out the light, which could deteriorate the chemicals inside. He wrapped the radio parts in several sheets of waxed paper and shoved one deep into one jar, and then put the others in other jars. He told no one, not even Naomi, what had happened.

Some number of months later, the man returned one late afternoon and collected the rectifier and other parts. Bob never found out his name.

Still later, there was a rumor that the Japanese were looking for a radio in the camp. Apparently some "news" from the outside had gotten around and the guards' suspicions were raised. One man was questioned intently and there was talk that the guards were looking for "Smitty," who was involved with the radio. Fortunately, there were a number of Smiths in the camp and after a while, like most of the other investigations, interest in finding "Smitty" died down. No one ever talked to Bob, and it was only after the war that he told Naomi what he had done.

The Other One

September 1943

The Chinese amah Kong came by the camp, stopping near the package line which was used by the internees to bring in food and other necessaries from the outside civilian Filipino population. It was the second visit she had made since the Smiths were interned. She sent in a message and then waited impassively, squatting in the summer heat near the front gate on the bustling tree-lined Espana Avenue while they found Naomi inside. Kong carried a green woven basket of palm-leaf fronds containing packaged quantities of rice, string-tied fresh green vegetables, a form of cabbage, and fruits sitting on a layer of four or five camotes, a kind of sweet potato. It was some time before Naomi came to the opening in the front fence which had been covered with sawali matting, a woven beige bamboo structure used to line the fence and control access. She was leading Bobby by the hand. Kong's face lit up, and the little boy squealed with delight when he saw her. They chattered through the fence opening for a time, an almost unintelligible conversation to Naomi, and then Kong moved over beside the package line entrance and pushed through the food basket. Naomi tried to give her some money, but she smiled and said: "For my Bobby." As an afterthought she added: "And how is the other one?" referring to the year-old boy she had never seen.

"He is doing better," Naomi said, trying to explain the situation. It was clear that Kong's English was not sufficient for her to comprehend fully and so Naomi finished: "He is fine." Kong left shortly after, and they never saw each other again, nor did Naomi ever hear what had happened to her.

"The other one," the second son, Billy, was at Santa Catalina Hospital across the road from the camp—a former convent/residence for nurses and Catholic sisters that had been commandeered by the Japanese and was used as an auxiliary hospital for the camp. It was on the opposite side of the street from the camp, with high wooden walls blocking the street so escape was discouraged, but more importantly, fraternization with the Filipino civilians was almost impossible.

Billy, at just over a year old, had been found crying in his crib, his leg painful and no indication of cause. The doctors at Santo Tomas infirmary isolated the issue to his left hip but no one knew what the problem was. It was nearly two days before a Filipino doctor diagnosed the problem as a septic hip, meaning a likely bacterial infection of the hip joint, causing the joint to separate, filling with fluid. How the infection started was a mystery. Unfortunately, there was little in the way of medication to treat it. Billy was moved to Santa Catalina, where the leg was immobilized and put in traction. A hollow needle was inserted to drain the hip of infectious fluid so the hip joint could reset into the socket. He was given the limited available medication for pain and fever. Naomi was at the hospital every day, returning to camp at curfew each evening.

One morning Naomi came to Billy's room and found he had kicked out the needle drain in the night. The Filipino doctor checked him and decided to leave it out. He told her it was "healing reasonably." He stood across the bed from her and said: "If he can walk, he will always drag his leg like this," making an exaggerated motion trailing his left leg behind him. "If I could have reached across that bed," Naomi said, "I would have strangled that doctor."

With the passage of time, Billy began to stand and bear weight on the leg. Naomi was worried he would damage it more, but her physician, Dr. Fletcher, said, "If it hurts him, he won't put any weight on it. Let him do it." Within three months, Billy was walking almost normally for a 15-month-old child, and after a time, running around with Bobby near the shanty. While the leg was always shorter, he seldom exhibited any signs of difficulty with it. However, cross country running was never a strong suit, although he became a happy but unremarkable skier in later life.

MS Gripsholm

Late Fall, 1943
Laurel, Delaware

Annie Bishop was in a tizzy. She had been contacted by the American Red Cross and given a tight timeline, as well as very specific instructions. She could send a package to her daughter in Santo Tomas if she got it done on time. Non-perishable food, medicines, personal articles, and clothes could be boxed up, given to the Red Cross, and they would be delivered to her interned family in Manila. Size and weight were tightly limited.

In 1942, the U.S. State Department had chartered the nearly 600-foot-long Swedish ocean liner *MS Gripsholm* to act as a repatriation conduit for diplomats of the warring powers and their families stranded by the war, either in the U.S. or elsewhere. The ship would take Japanese, Germans, or Italians to a neutral port, often Portugal, where they would be exchanged for American, Canadian, or other British Empire diplomats and their families. The ship would be manned by Swedish officers and crew and under the control of the International Red Cross. The *Gripsholm* was painted white, highlighted by two blue diagonal stripes, with the nearly 10-foot-tall word "Sverige" (Sweden) and the smaller word "Diplomat" on both sides. The liner could carry nearly 2,000 passengers. During 1942 and 1943, it made numerous trips across the Atlantic and then later the Pacific. In 1943, an agreement was reached under the urging of the Red

Cross to allow supplies to be sent to Allied civilian internees in Axis internee camps via the *Gripsholm* as it went about its repatriation and diplomatic voyages.

The American Red Cross contacted the families of internees of whom they had record. But once agreement was gained to send packages to the camps, then time was of the essence as the ship was sailing on a pre-set course, known to all the warring powers, from New York (via Rio de Janeiro), then across the Atlantic around South Africa to Portuguese India, and then through the Indian Ocean via the Philippines, and on to Japan. The route was cleared in advance by the warring parties so the *Gripsholm* could travel in relative safety.

Annie packed and repacked the box to the limit of size and weight she had been given, trying to guess what her daughter and grandsons would need but with no real knowledge of their situation and no time or way to contact them. Weight was a concern, so she rejected canned milk for powdered milk; limited clothes she sent to underwear (it was hot in the tropics, wasn't it?), omitted simple medicines like aspirin, but then stuck in a small supply of what her neighbor, the pharmacist Dr. Williams, recommended. It was so hard to choose. But she made the schedule and the supplies were sent.

Earlier in 1942, just after they were interned, Naomi had worried about the future and what they would do. She was a planner. "Bobby is a year old and the new baby is coming soon," she had told Bob. "We need formula … milk … for them. And we should get some supplies while we can." Bob was working in the camp pharmacy and hospital several hours a day. He ran the pharmacy and so was given occasional passes into Manila and money from the Camp Committee to buy supplies. On one of his trips, he made contact with some Filipinos who had worked with him before the war. They got him some carnation and pet evaporated milk and other supplies, which he stashed in the pharmacy, away from the other internees housed with his family. Later, Naomi watered it down and gave it to the children after sources available through the camp officials began to dry up. It was a godsend. The *Gripsholm* box would be a much-needed bridge.

In 1945, in a rare letter home to the Bishops in Laurel, Bob wrote: "We received intact your package sent on the *Gripsholm,* and you'll never realize how much it meant to us." In her school book chronology, Naomi records: "Dec. 15 (1943) American relief supplies arrive." She does not mention the *Gripsholm,* but based on the timing that had to be the source.

Bob continued in his letter: "The only American Red Cross Comfort Kits we received were those which came back on the *Gripsholm.* They were literally life savers. The first year we had a small kit from South Africa, and the second year, one from Canada, and those are the only relief supplies of any kind that we have received in these three years." Naomi records those in her chronology as December 17, 1942 …"South African relief supplies arrive," and January 6, 1943 … "Canadian relief supplies arrive."

Sunday Dinner

Laurel, Delaware
January 1943

Laurel, Delaware was a town of less than 3,000 souls in the 1940s, actually smaller in population than the Santo Tomas Internment Camp. It is situated on Broad Creek in the far southwest corner of the small state, only some 20 odd miles from Salisbury, Maryland. The town supported the local farming community.

Chickens were the big business, with townspeople fattening birds under contract to Swift or other producers. A large feed mill was situated beyond the empty field behind the Bishop home on Central Avenue, which is the main street in town, with the high school on one side and homes along the other. The gray stone Grace Methodist Church sits on Central Avenue only two doors from the Lutheran Church, about a block beyond Spicer's Market on the main square and four blocks from the high school. Many of the streets are tree-lined, and many homes have white picket fences, or black wrought iron ones, separating the yards from the sidewalks.

Annie Bishop took off her hat and put it on top of the dresser. She changed from her church dress to a slightly faded pale-blue gingham house dress. It was warm for January, so she didn't put her corset back on. She would be described as stout by anyone honest, with graying hair held under a pale hairnet and rimless glasses. She shook herself slightly—"Good to be easy now," she thought. Below, she heard the door close and footsteps on the stairs. George came into the bedroom, sat on the side of the bed, and removed his shoes. He was thin, tall, balding, and gray, with a bad back from an accident years earlier at the saw mill.

"I'll get a chicken," she said. "Maybe Grace and Doc can come over for dinner."

"Fine," he said.

Downstairs, she paused by the desk in the hall at the foot of the staircase. Beside the black telephone was the Red Cross postcard. She picked it up. It was only the second one they had received since the "chil'ren" had been interned in the prisoner of war camp in Manila. She thought of her daughter, a woman, not a child, who was just 37 years old at her last birthday, and the husband they only knew through photos, and the two children they had never seen either—one now just six months old and the other just two plus years.

Only the standard limit of 25 words was on the card, and even though Naomi had tightened her ideas as brief as she could, still the message was scanty. "We're in good health," it said. "Kids are growing well. Food was poorly, though adequate, but a Red Cross package had come. Write. Will myself soon. Love. Signature."

The first post card, sent through the auspices of the American Red Cross, had been even more terse. The young family had been interned by the Japanese in February, 1942, at the University of Santo Tomas in Manila. Immediately, Annie had sent a reply, but now, months later, they finally had some word. She put the postcard back down on the table.

Looking at it always triggered thoughts of that brief, concise War Department telegram in December 1942 about her youngest son, Billy. "We regret to inform you that Lt. James William Bishop is missing in action." Nothing more.

He was often in her mind—her youngest son, always called "Billy," a 1937 graduate of the University of Maryland, College of Agriculture. He had been 21 years old at the graduation, handsome in cap and gown, and so excited to see the world. After graduation, he signed on as crew on the Baltimore Mail Line, a steamship company with a five-ship fleet, sailing from Baltimore to Norfolk, then Le Havre, France, and finally Hamburg, Germany, and return with weekly mail, cargo, and passenger service, but only about 80 passengers. He crewed on several voyages until the company went bust in late 1938 and was acquired by the Panama Pacific Line. He left the world of the sea and joined with his father in a chicken farming venture on Rehoboth Bay, Delaware. Having sailed the world, he found chickens boring. In January 1941, well before Pearl Harbor, he joined the army, signing up for flight training and ultimately becoming a bomber pilot.

The War Department telegram in December 1942 had been a blow. Billy had first been assigned to flight training in the southern United States. In early 1942, age 26, he was posted to England, where he trained for another five months. He was among the first to land in Casablanca with his crew as part of the Operation Torch invasion. Later, the family found he had been flying his B-25 in North Africa.

First, the postcard from the Red Cross about Naomi and her family, and then the War Department telegram about Billy. "It was more than a body could bear," she had thought ... her youngest and her oldest. Later in December 1943, Billy Bishop was reclassified from missing in action to killed in action. Despite inquiries, the Army never told them how or where. She didn't tell Naomi about her brother.

Annie put on a coat, went through the kitchen, out the back door, and across the yard to the chicken coop, situated behind and to the left of the two-car garage. She selected one of the less productive layers, scooped it up and wrung its neck. The hen still kicked but soon was still. Unconsciously, she stroked it, walking back toward the rear stoop. A big pecan tree, nearly 25 feet tall, stood by the stoop, providing summer shade.

Toward the fence, two large apple trees sprawled into the grass in the yard. The air was cool, and it was still on a Sunday morning. She sat on the stoop and plucked the chicken.

George came out on the stoop, thin, 67 years old, slightly bent and favoring his always-bad back.

"I'm going into the office for a couple of hours."

"Would you stop and invite the Williamses? I think I saw Grace when I was going out to the coop."

He nodded. Grace and Doc Williams lived next door. They were the best of good neighbors and they had lived side by side for nearly 20 years. The houses were set back comfortably from the front sidewalk—big white two-story buildings with wide cool verandas protecting the front from the street and large evergreen junipers lining the porch. They were directly across from the high school on Central Avenue. George would walk to his office, what with gas rationing. He went in many weekends. His business, Townsend and Bishop lumber and building supplies, had failed in the Depression. They had filed for bankruptcy, and Townsend had left town shortly after. But George had restarted the business, brokering lumber and wood and also reselling. He had continued to pay their old creditors. It had taken nine years, but he had paid all the debts of the old company. He didn't have to, but he paid them. He had grown accustomed to working six days or more a week.

He stopped next door. Grace Williams answered his knock; she was a trim, tall, straight-backed woman with rimless glasses, gray hair, shiny, with a Marcel curl, nearly the opposite of Annie, who was stout, short, and wore her hair in a bun. "I just walk by a plate of food and gain five pounds," she once told Grace. Of course, the ladies of the Methodist Church acknowledged that she was likely the best cook in Sussex County.

"Delighted," Grace said to the invitation. "I'll bring a corn pudding."

"Around four," he said. "Come early, and we'll talk a while."

Annie prepared the chicken, buttering the skin very lightly. She used to lavish butter on a roasting chicken, but since the war, she served it "natural," as she said. Later, she went into the cellar and got some preserved peaches for a pie, a jar of pickles, and a jar of canned beans. She picked three good potatoes as well.

George came back from his office near 3:15 p.m., the house smelling lovely of roasted chicken and the spicy smell of peach pie. He went to the kitchen, got a glass, and poured bourbon into it, about two fingers. Annie looked up disapproving, but said nothing. It did no good anyway. She recalled when he had come back from a difficult day in Dover several years earlier and she had been entertaining the ladies of the Women's Christian Temperance Union in the parlor. He had said good evening to the WCTU committee as he came in, went into the kitchen, and poured himself a drink, bourbon as usual. He sat at the kitchen table with this week's copy of *The State Register*, reading it. She had hurried into the kitchen and asked him not to drink just now, but he explained it had been a difficult day, and if she would keep the committee in the parlor, everything would be all right. Flustered, she had gone back to the ladies, and he had resumed reading.

Doc Williams was one of three pharmacists in town. He and Grace arrived just after George got back from his office. Grace went through to the kitchen with her pudding, and George poured Doc a drink. They were Episcopalians, so of course saw nothing wrong with a taste of bourbon from time to time. The two men sat on the porch talking about the war and business and the town. George lit his pipe.

Annie showed Grace the Red Cross postcard.

"It's a mercy you have some word," Grace said. "And they sound all right."

Annie nodded. "But you still worry. They can tell you so little. And those babies, it must be a nightmare for her." Grace helped with the potatoes, mashing them with a little butter and milk instead of cream. Annie made the gravy while the chicken rested. She called the men in from the porch. Grace poured iced tea for everyone.

The heavy mahogany dining table was covered with a clean, white cloth, chased around by pastel blue, green, and pink embroidery. Grace and Annie set the food on the table, the chicken in front of George to carve. Expertly he disassembled the bird, putting generous portions on each plate. They passed the green beans, potatoes, and pudding. George asked the blessing.

They began to eat. George paused, stopping at the second mouthful of chicken.

He pushed his plate away. "I just can't eat," he said, "thinking of those children in that camp. I just don't have any appetite." He stood up and walked out to the porch, taking his pipe from the parlor side table. Annie looked at Grace and Doc.

"I know how he feels," she said. "But he'll be all right. And it won't do them any good if we waste this dinner." The three finished their meal with quiet talk of life in Laurel, friends and such. Grace and Annie cleaned up the table, and Doc went out to the porch.

"I'm sorry," George said. "I hope I didn't ruin your dinner."

"Don't give it another thought," Doc said. "It's the times." He sat beside George in a high-back wooden rocker, moving slightly.

"I expect this is the most comfortable porch in Laurel," Doc said. "It's always so lovely and fine, especially on a day like this." They rocked quietly together. Soon Grace and Annie came out and joined them. She handed George a glass of iced tea. He sipped it.

Near seven, Grace and Doc went home to listen to Jack Benny on the radio.

They were big fans. Annie went into the kitchen. In a few moments, George followed.

"I kept your dinner warm in the oven. See if you feel like eating a little. It's a shame to let it go to waste in times like these." He sat at the kitchen table and ate a small amount.

"You know what I'd like?" he asked. Annie shook her head. "A piece of your peach pie." She smiled and cut him one.

"I'm sorry," he said. "I didn't mean to ruin your dinner."

"I know," she said. "Everything will work out all right."

Schooling

Early 1942
Santo Tomas

There were many children in the camp, ranging in age from new-borns to late teens. Early in the internment, the Camp Executive Committee set up a system of school classes as close as possible to what would have been found pre-war. Naomi recorded that "approximately 700 children and young people from primary to college grades (were in school) operated by permission but with no help from Japanese." She continued:

"Similar number of persons attended special adult classes until prohibited in early 1944," after the Japanese assumed actual operation of the camp.

Of course, most students before the war went to private schools, their parents often being well-to-do or at least wanting to keep up appearances. Americans married to Filipinas were interned, but mostly their wives and children were not.

The internees encompassed a wide spectrum of experience, education, and skills.

Bob was asked to teach a class in chemistry. Chemistry he knew, but teaching and teen-agers were not his strong suit. Mary Alice was an older teen, about 16 when they were interned, and she was assigned to his class. Later, she admitted that she learned almost nothing about chemistry, but Bob would tutor her after classes to try to help, and they grew close, later teaching her to play bridge. Also, she often babysat Bobby or Billy for Naomi. She whispered her teenage dreams and secrets to the three-month-old baby. He never told a soul what she said.

One of the school teens, a couple of years older than Mary Alice, was a boy, Len Baker from England, a buddy of Mary Alice's. Len was fascinated by the lessons in chemistry, and Bob gave him a job after school in the laboratory he oversaw. The teen would clean beakers, flasks, and such, as well as arrange the chemicals in their glass jars as Bob directed, sweep, and tidy up. Bob even let him help distill some 'special fluid' for adult use. Len loved it all. Later after the war, he would study chemistry at university and go on to a successful career, settling in Wales.

Mary Alice recalls those school days: "In late January 1942, makeshift school classes were started. I imagine the initial thought was to keep us busy, but in the end, it saved us from falling three years behind. The majority of teachers and students from various pre-war schools were all in camp … all we lacked were books and supplies. But our teachers taught us with what they had: their brain power and initiative. I graduated from high school on April 30, 1943 with an appropriate diploma and grade re-sults acceptable to colleges after the war. In addition, we learned from specialists in many fields and perhaps had wider exposure to many careers than many of our peer groups elsewhere."

The camp had received a supply of books early in the war from the YMCA, and as Mary Alice said, they were "read and reread" by many in the camp beyond the school children.

The height of the "school year" was the follies put on by the students. Everyone in the camp came to the makeshift stage and watched as amateur singers, dancers, comedians, and musicians did their best. Len Baker and Mary Alice appeared in the camp "college show" performing a duet called "Home Cookin' Mama," appar-ently to rousing applause. In an earlier follies show, they had done the unforgettable song "Behind the Sawali," the lyrics to which have apparently vanished. Even some of the Japanese soldiers would watch, standing in the back amazed at what the prisoners would do to amuse themselves. Later in 1944, when food and energy had been diminished, the extra-curricular activities slowly ended.

Shopping

Manila
July, 1943

Jesus Leonidez walked along Avenida Espana looking through the bars of the iron fence which separated Santo Tomas University from the bustling city street. A handsome, well-groomed man with slicked-back black hair and a traditional pale beige banana cloth shirt, he blended into the crowd on the street. Carefully, he watched to see if Bob was there. Some days earlier, his wife had gotten a small, half-page message with a few pesos from Naomi. On one side of the little piece of paper was a list of things she wanted Josefina to buy—some Life Buoy soap, cooking oil, toilet paper, and other necessaries. But on the back, it said simply "Jesus Tuesday." And so here on Tuesday, Jesus was standing outside the internment camp. He passed the guard not looking into the camp, but across the street and not walking too fast or too slow. On the second circuit, he saw Bob at the fence and walked over to him.

"I have a pass for tomorrow. We will need some medical supplies and some things for the lab. Can you arrange for entertainment for the guard?"

"Yes."

"Is it all right? You got the other message?"

"Sir, yes, it is all right."

"Okay. I'll see you then. Thanks."

Bob smiled, and Jesus nodded. Jesus had been a key manager for Glo-Co, the pharmaceutical company where Bob was secretary-treasurer. Several times, they had traveled to the provinces together when there were some credit or payment issues with customers, and Jesus needed help. Once they had spent three days together living in a rural hotel after a Glo-Co delivery truck had gone off the narrow, paved road into a deep water-filled ditch half way to Batangas, outside Manila. Bob and Jesus had been sent to arrange to pull the van out of the ditch and they had become friendly. Jesus was amazed that Bob lived in the same primitive rural hotel he did on the trip. After Bob and Naomi were interned in Santo Tomas, Jesus had sent word through the fence and had begun buying supplies for them on the market in Manila with money Bob had given him. Naomi was concerned, especially for milk for the children, and started putting in a reserve stock of various supplies, mostly canned goods, which Bob stashed in the lab, there being no place to keep them safely in the dormitory areas.

Wednesday, Jesus was there outside the fence with a bicycle rickshaw. Bob followed the Japanese guard out of the gate and the guard stopped, suspicious. He turned and looked at Bob, who smiled and gestured toward the rickshaw. The guard was a peasant from a village in the mountains in the north of Japan. He hated the heat and humidity of Manila and simply wished to be home. Out of the sight of his officers he carried his rifle like a fat stick, held in the middle. With a grunt he climbed into the rickshaw, and Bob slid in beside him, smiling again. Jesus trotted alongside as they moved into the busy street.

The guard looked ahead impassively as they moved through the city traffic, finally stopping at a bar on the corner of an awning-covered street filled with stalls and shopping Filipinos. Bob was surprised at the amount of commerce still going on. Behind the fence in the camp, everything had changed for the internees, but here on the street, life went on. There were fewer goods on the shelves and in the bins, and the prices had gone up considerably, but still, there was food and the common goods of life. Bob signaled to the guard to get out and the three of them went into the bar. Jesus ordered San Miguel beer and the guard sat at a table near the door while Bob and Jesus sat further inside the bar, within sight of the guard, but some distance away. Placidly, the guard drank his beer, looking at nothing in particular and lost in his own thoughts. In a few minutes, he signaled for another beer, which was brought to him promptly. The side of the bar was open to the street, and a breeze slightly cooled the place. Two fans turned lazily overhead. It was fairly dark in the bar, with the only light, except for a fixture over the bar counter, coming from the open-air windows on the street side. Jesus and Bob watched the guard for a while and made sure a third beer was brought to him. Jesus turned and looked at an elderly Filipino man by the cash register, who nodded at a woman leaning against a corner of the bar. Bob got up and walked over to the guard, the woman coming over beside him. Bob pointed to the stairs and the woman and gestured to the guard. Knowing the guard spoke no English, still he said, "You want to go upstairs?" The guard nodded and smiled, then propped his rifle against the wall beside the table, picked up his San Miguel, and tromped up the stairs. Two more beers were sent up to the room.

When Bob returned to the table, there were two more men sitting with Jesus. He looked from one to the other. "Sir, these are men from the company. Very trustworthy." Bob recognized one of them from the warehouse. The other he didn't know. He nodded and sat down.

Nothing was in writing except a list of pharmaceuticals and chemicals that were needed. The list bore the mark of the camp commandant's office authorizing the purchase on behalf of the Internee Committee. One of the men took the list and left the bar. Quietly, Bob gave the other two the memorized message which had some kind of code in it. The other man nodded and left. Jesus ordered two more beers, and they waited.

Bob did not know what was going on exactly, and he didn't want to know. Some kind of message was requested by the Internee Committee, a reply for which would be put in the false bottom of the wooden boxes transporting the chemicals. The hollow area would be less than half an inch, undetectable from the outside, but a secure hiding place for folded paper. Bob suspected the communication was between American Army officers hiding in the jungle in the north of Manila and the camp officials. He never found out what was involved and never asked.

In time, the woman came down from the room upstairs. "He wants whisky," she said. She smiled. "And I want a bath." Bob nodded, and Jesus went to the bar. The female bartender took down a half empty bottle of scotch, uncorked it, and spit into the bottle, re-corking it, and then carefully shaking it to mix the saliva. She smiled and handed it to Jesus, who took it up to the guard.

It was nearly an hour before the two men sent to buy the goods returned. They had brought back with them a small four-wheel cart with the wooden cases filled with the chemicals and three additional boxes containing the things needed by the hospital. Jesus ordered beer for everyone and they talked quietly for a few minutes. Bob thanked them and handed over the money he had brought for the drugs. The men tried to refuse, but Jesus insisted that the transaction had to be "normal," and so they took the money and left, bowing and smiling.

Upstairs, the guard was half drunk. He had been crying and softly singing a Japanese love song to himself. He was out of uniform, sitting in his underwear. Somehow, he had managed to let the woman know he was a farmer and just wanted to go home. "I'd like him to go home, too," she told Bob, shaking her head slightly. Bob, Jesus, and the woman helped him to dress. He was compliant, cooperative, and smiled at the woman, attempting to fondle her again, but she skillfully dodged his hands, and he lost interest.

Once dressed, they got him downstairs with some difficulty and into the back of the cart, where he sat leaning against one of the crates. Bob handed him his rifle, which he put on the floor of the cart beside himself. Then, apparently remembering his position, he pulled himself up and looked around and smiled at the passers-by.

The ride back to the camp was quicker than the ride out had been. It was well after lunch and siesta time for the Filipinos.

Bob and Jesus stopped the cart some distance before the gate to the camp and the guard got out. He started to walk to the camp, but Jesus stopped him and handed him his rifle. At the gate, the guard stood to the side and Bob showed his pass to the sergeant there, who looked over the cart and then at the list Bob had given him. His attention turned to the guard, who was unsteady on his feet, and then he looked back at Bob, who shrugged. The sergeant waved Bob through with the cart, but stopped Jesus, who quietly turned and walked away. Bob continued on, pushing the cart. The sergeant then turned on the guard and berated him, slapping his face and yelling in Japanese while the guard stood at attention, sobering up quickly.

As instructed, Bob took the cart to the lab, assisted by three internees who had materialized from the sidelines somehow. "Let us give you a hand," one said. Bob nodded and went off to have a smoke. Later, he went up to the lab. The chemicals had been unloaded from the crates and were on the lab counter and floor. The crates were gone. Bob put the jars of chemicals away in their proper places, looked around the lab, and then went out, locking the door behind him, to find Naomi.

Shanties

June, 1942
Santo Tomas

Americans have a tendency to be innovative and inventive people. The camp was crowded. Families were split up with the men and older boys in one building and the women, girls, and young children in another. The university campus was a large sprawling place, and someone came up with the idea of using some free space in the open patios inside the main buildings, or beside them, to construct nipa huts made of bamboo and a covering of palm fronds. Also, space outside the buildings was used later for additional shanties. Some available arable ground was already being used to grow food, which was expanded year by year as the internment continued. In the hot tropical days, the shanties would provide relief and a place for families and friends to find a kind of relative privacy and a chance to be together. The camp committee liked the idea, and the Japanese did not object. There were rules, of course, like having clear views into and through each shanty so there could be no secret goings-on. Sex was one of the "goings on" in the minds of the camp officials, and the "see through" policy was central to that control. It only worked partly. Surely poor nutrition after a time was a more potent control factor for most activities.

Bob immediately signed up for a shanty and invited the Foleys to join in. By using it for two families, the camp committee felt better about the process, and theirs was one of the earliest approved. After it was built, Bob asked Jesus one day at the front fence if he could get a small banana tree. The next time Bob had to go out to buy chemicals and drugs, Jesus showed him some banana trees and Bob chose one—not too large, he was told, which they took back to the camp.

Bob planted it next to the shanty.

"Silly," one man said. "It takes nearly 15 months before that tree will bear fruit. We'll be out of here long before that ... probably by Christmas." Bob smiled and nodded. Why argue? In due course, the banana tree had set fruit, and Bob proudly picked some bananas and gave them to Naomi. She peeled them and broke them apart for the two boys. To her surprise, inside were large seeds the size of watermelon seeds.

"Bob, look." He stared at the banana, then took a piece and tasted it. Little did he know that there were many varieties of bananas, and not all were like those familiar from home.

"Tastes fine."

She sighed and began digging out the seeds, giving the boys the mushy banana which they loved. For the balance of internment while the tree produced, she picked out seeds from smallish but very sweet bananas. Likely the work involved in getting any fruit kept others from stealing very many of their bananas.

"Well, I guess I am a better forecaster than a botanist," Bob would say. Naomi would just smile since she was the one digging out the seeds.

The shanty, even though crowded in amongst other shanties, was a kind of refuge from the constant coming and going, talking, and yelling in the main dormitory areas of the buildings. Naomi records that there were 683 shanties housing 1,108 people, built in the camp, according to figures published at the time of liberation. The boys would play around the shanty, with whatever games children devise. They also had their cat as company. And the Foleys spent time there as well when they were not working or in school.

Naomi recalled sitting with Ella Foley, quietly watching the children, when for once, neither of them had any pressing chores to do. "You'll think I'm crazy," Ella said softly, a woman closer to 60 than 40. She looked over at Naomi. "I could get used to this life."

Naomi stared at her a long moment. "I mean," Ella said, "there is no responsibility. There's nothing you can do. You do what you're told; you take care of your family. There is no pushing to get ahead or worry about what you have or don't have. There are no bills to pay. You just exist in limbo." She paused: "I told you you'd think I was crazy." Of course, later when food was poor and scarce, Ella likely would not have had that particular thought. But early in the war, with supplies still available from Manila, such thoughts did creep in. People deal with adversity in many ways.

One day at the shanty, Naomi was cleaning the bum of one of the boys after he had "done his duty." She used pages from old pharmacy prescription pads that Bob had "borrowed" from the hospital. There was nothing to prescribe in the dispensary or the hospital, so the pads were useless for their intended purpose. Bob mentioned them and Naomi immediately saw the benefit. As the war dragged on, she began tearing the prescription forms in half to conserve her supply of kiddie toilet paper. Her friend Madge Gelbwaks stood watching the process. "Well, after the war," Madge said, "at least you'll have a use for cancelled postage stamps."

After the shanty was first built, a Catholic priest, Father John Sheehan—a friend and pastor to the Foleys—came by one afternoon some months later. He had a small Kodak box camera with him.

"I'll just take a couple of quick snaps," he said, wandering around the shanty photographing Bobby and Billy.

It was high risk. Just *having* a camera was a punishable offense and likely would entail a severe beating by the Japanese. Taking pictures was worse. You could be shot. After a short time, the Father left. They would see him from time to time, but he never said a word. When the camp was liberated in 1945, Father Sheehan came by to see Naomi. He handed her a roll of film.

"Hope it's okay," he said. "It's been buried these many months."

She got the film developed, and although the pictures are fuzzy, they are the only ones of the boys from that time, except for one Japanese-approved photo, believed to be for propaganda purposes, taken of each child. In a few days, the priest was repatriated back to the States, and the Smiths never saw him again.

Fine Dining

Early 1944

Since mid-1943, the war had been progressively deteriorating for the Japanese across their wide Pacific and Asian "empire." The Philippines had been lying far behind the "front lines" in the Pacific war for nearly two years, but now the islands became likely invasion targets on the road to Japan. In this war environment, the Japanese Imperial Army in Manila dismissed the Santo Tomas camp internee executive committee and assumed the actual operation of Santo Tomas shortly after the beginning of February 1944. Life in the camp got worse immediately and declined continuously until liberation. Naomi notes the date and event: "Feb. 1 ... Military administration takes over camp. Filipino doctors and nurses, also market vendors, barred. Daily cereal ration 400 grams per person per day." The next entry: "Feb. 7 ... Package line closed," which was the way internees could receive things from outside. Then on Feb. 20 she notes: "Military takes over (camp) bodega and all food supplies therein." Japanese troops now walked patrols around the camp perimeter and along the walls of the university, something they had rarely done before. Contact between the internees and the Filipinos and neutrals outside was severely restricted, and exchanges and vendors were prohibited inside and out. Food was only available from the central kitchen and the quantity and quality diminished noticeably. Nearly one internee in five was over 60 years of age, and they began to suffer almost immediately from starvation and various diseases related to lack of nutrition, such as beriberi and rickets. The death rate, especially for older internees, rose materially.

Naomi recorded the decline in food after the Japanese took over management of the camp. She wrote: "Feb. 1, Military Administration takes over camp … Daily cereal ration 400 grams per person per day." And: "Sept. 13, Daily cereal ration 250 grams. Sept. 15, Daily cereal ration 200 grams. Sept. 20, Daily cereal ration 300 grams." She noted on Sept. 23: "Produce for vegetable market so reduced that market at last closes." Earlier on August 1, the Japanese confiscated all money from internees, except for the Japanese 50 peso script, and ordered that the money be deposited with the Bank of Taiwan, that island nation being a "protectorate" of Japan.

On November 17, the daily cereal ration was cut to 255 grams, then on December 12 to 210 grams, and on December 20 to 187 grams per person per day. As Naomi said at the time: "Happy Christmas 1944 from the Emperor of Japan."

When food was available, it was unaffordable; Naomi wrote a list of prices for commodities in the camp, when available, as of December 31, 1944. The list which she attributes to Peter Richard of No. 6 Uli Uli, San Miguel, Manila, P.I., is as follows:

Commodity	Price in Equivalent U.S. $
Sugar (kilo)	$105
Rice (kilo)	60
Corned beef (12 oz can)	40
Evap. milk (14 oz can)	20
Margarine (pound)	90
Vegetable lard (pound)	90
Unrefined coconut oil (Quart)	70
Smoking tobacco (1/4 kilo)	40

For comparison, in 1945, the average annual wage in the U.S. was $2,400, with the minimum wage set at 40 cents an hour.

House rent in the U.S. averaged $60 a month, bread was nine cents a loaf, milk 62 cents a gallon, and a man's shirt cost $2.50.

Of course, with nearly 4,000 people in the camp, there were wide discrepancies in health and well-being amongst the population. Older, poorer people suffered most after the military took over running the camp and began cutting rations. Younger internees, particularly those who had money and contacts in the city, did materially better. If you look at photos of the internees at liberation, some of the people are just skin and bones and others thin, but more normally proportioned. The starvation became palpable as 1944 progressed under Japanese operation of the camp. Some internees could barely walk up the flights of stairs in the buildings to their beds.

In Santo Tomas, as time went by, food was the never-ending topic of conversation—the constant concern and the constant worry. As the war crawled on, people would sit together, and while chatting, almost always bring the conversation to some past dinner or meal or celebration that they would then describe in detail: what they ate, how it was prepared, and how good it was. Food was communal in the sense that the Japanese now provided certain amounts which were distributed to everyone, resulting in longer lines and bland, uninteresting offerings, soupy rice and garlic, sweet potatoes called comates, various greens of dubious nutritional value, which deteriorated even more as the war continued. On June 6, 1944, Naomi recorded in her chronology: "Central kitchen starts cooking in outside kitchen permanently with wood." Earlier in the internment in late 1942, the Japanese had put sawali mats woven of local fronds along the university fence on Espana Avenue to control contact between internees and the local populace. Now they were adding even more mats to end virtually all food commerce. By the liberation of the camp after three years' imprisonment, Bob and Naomi each weighed around 100 pounds, having lost 20-45 pounds. Mary Alice reported that at internment, she weighed 164 pounds, and was down to 124 by liberation. However, both children were well and actually slightly fat, being the recipients of the best of what was available, and Naomi's prudence in secretly setting aside some articles from food packages like the *Gripsholm* supplies. In the last months before liberation, Naomi even resorted to boiling leaves and stems from palm trees on her charcoal cooker in the shanty to give some substance to their meals, although there was virtually no nutrition in it.

Naomi records toward the end of her schoolbook chronology that the internee average loss of weight from the beginning of internment in January 1942 up to August 15, 1944 (just six months after the Japanese took over control) was 27 pounds for men and 16 pounds for women. From August 1944 to January 20, 1945, just before liberation on February 3, the loss was an additional 24 pounds for men and 16 pounds for women. For both men and women, virtually the same weight was lost by internees in the five months from August 15, 1944 to liberation as in the entire 32-month period between January 1942 internment and mid-August 1944. The clear difference: the Japanese military in February 1944 took control of the food supply from the internee committee.

It was said: "In the first year of the war, if you found a bug in your rice, you threw the whole bowl away. In the second year, you just threw the bug away, and in the third year, you ate the bug, too."

The Cat in the Camp

Santo Tomas
September 1944

He was usually called simply "the cat," but Billy called him "Bootie" some of the time. He was a non-descript calico, brown and white, and had simply appeared one day, as cats sometimes do. On his way somewhere, he had decided to stay until it served his purpose to get on with his plan. Early in the war, there had been a few pets in the camp, brought by people who didn't know what to do with them, but slowly they disappeared. The cat took care of himself. He slept in the shanty and hunted lizards, birds and mice, rather successfully. Starvation was not in his plans.

Both of the boys treated him like part of the family. He allowed himself to be petted—when it suited him—and he slept on one of the cots in the shanty throughout most of the hot days, hunting at night. Probably he would look for lady cats in the camp, but it was a vain search.

"I just don't know how you can keep a cat in a camp," Maria (her last name is not important) said to Naomi one day. Maria and her husband Otto were Dutch, or maybe Danish. They had lived in Manila for many years and had not been picked up at the start of the war since the Japanese apparently confused them with neutrals, possibly Swiss. But for reasons none clearly understood, the Japanese had finally interned them in late 1943. Protests seemed to have no impact. Maria complained about it to anyone who would listen. She was a tall, spare, gray-haired woman, often querulous, and as a result, not particularly pleasant company.

Otto and Maria were housed separately in the camp; he with the men and she in the Administration Building with the women and children, one floor down from Naomi and the boys, who had moved from the Annex earlier. But the couple had money and had fairly quickly acquired a shanty not far from Bob and Naomi's. So, to speak, they were neighbors. Their children were grown and had been at school in Switzerland when the war broke out. They hadn't seen them in over three years.

"We should have gone home," she often said. "I wanted to go home, but Otto wouldn't." She would pause and look away. "We should have gone home right away." Her English was sort of German accented, since they had lived in Zurich many years.

"It is not right to have a cat here," she would say, standing by the banana tree outside the Smith shanty. Whenever they talked, the subject always came up. Naomi would smile and repeat what she always said. "Well, the boys like him and he really takes care of himself. It's no bother."

"A cat does not belong in a camp," Maria would repeat. "Send him to your amah or someone in Manila you know well. It would be better." Naomi would smile and change the subject. After nearly a half year of this same conversation, she simply ignored it.

The cat was independent, as cats are. Sometimes he would not come back from his hunting for a day or even two. But in late September, he was gone for several days. The boys began to whine, pestering Naomi about the cat. She put them off and finally had to admit that maybe the cat had just run away. The boys were downcast, but over time, thought less and less of him.

"Strange about that old cat," Bob said one evening. Naomi looked over at him.

After a long pause she said, "They ate him. Maria and Otto ate him. I know. Maria came by several days ago and offered me some of the meat. 'It's your cat, you should have some.' That's what she said." Bob took a drag on his homemade cigarette and shook his head.

"You know what else she said?" Naomi asked. He shook his head again. "She said, 'A cat does not belong in a camp.' She said we had no right to keep it, and they were hungry."

"Have you told the boys?"

"No. I'll wait until they are older."

Pennies

Even before the actual landings on Luzon Island by MacArthur's forces, Allied air forces began coming over the city, bombing key military or transportation points held by the Japanese, followed some weeks after by landings on beaches to the northwest of Manila. Some bombs went astray, and anti-aircraft shells fell indiscriminately, some into the camp. It was a difficult time for the internees, starving and being shelled. Naomi propped mattresses against a wall in the Annex, and when the planes came over, ordered the two boys to shelter behind them. There was no whining and no tantrums. You did as you were told, or possible spankings followed. It was possibly life or death.

During the war, announcements were made over the camp public address system to keep all internees informed of assemblies or things that needed doing. Of course, there was no "news" or announcements about the war. Sometimes there was music, which Bobby greatly enjoyed. The Japanese let the internee committee run the announcements and the PA system.

After the first bombing of Manila, someone (no one ever said who) put a record on the PA system. It was Bing Crosby singing the hit song "Pennies from Heaven." Some people noticed and looked at one another, smiling. But then it was played again. Some Japanese officer who spoke English finally realized what the song said and the PA was cut off.

"... if you want the things you love, you gotta have showers ...
... so when you hear it thunder, don't run under a tree ...
... there'll be pennies from heaven for you and me ..."

*Used by permission of **Alfred Music***

Debate

Honolulu
Summer 1944

There was no certainty that the Philippines would be liberated before the war ended. Early in the Pacific campaign in 1942, Roosevelt had split the command of Pacific Forces: the navy, under command of Admiral Chester Nimitz, in an island-hopping campaign, would charge across the Central Pacific, while the Army, under command of General MacArthur, would slog up from Australia along the Southeast Asian coast of New Guinea and the Philippines.

Now, by 1944, with demands for more and more war material coming from Russia and General Eisenhower in Europe, the issue of the Pacific focus for 1944-1945 could not be ignored. Roosevelt scheduled a meeting in a luxurious mansion on Waikiki Beach for early summer 1944. Nimitz, with his boss Admiral Ernest King, chief of naval operations, would meet with Douglas MacArthur in Honolulu to thrash out the strategy for the coming months. Roosevelt would attend as chairman and final decision-maker.

The debate was between (1) a strategy to end the Japan war as quickly as possible and (2) a global pan-Asian grand strategy to secure America's role in Asia after the war. From a military point of view, Nimitz's naval strategy of cross-Pacific attack likely would carry the day in any war college, a short and tough attack directly at Japan, but by-passing the Philippines. MacArthur, whose father, a career Army officer, had commanded in the Philippines in the early 20th century, and who himself was generalissimo of the Army of the Commonwealth of the Philippines, cared less for the quickest end to the Pacific war and more about the future of America in Asia. He argued that if America bypassed the islands—and abandoned the 17 million Filipinos, the thousands of Allied civilian prisoners of war, and military prisoners of war in the islands—the future would be bleak for Asian trust in U.S. commitments for decades to come.

Roosevelt had his own strategic issues. The presidential election for 1944 was fast approaching, and he had been nominated for a fourth term by the Democrats just days before he sailed for Honolulu. MacArthur's name had been mentioned in Republican circles, and newspapers such as *The Chicago Tribune,* as a possible Republican presidential candidate in that election. To abandon the Philippines and the American civilian internee hostages and former military held as prisoners of war by the Japanese would hand the very popular ("I shall return") MacArthur and the Republicans a massive mallet with which to beat Democrats, and especially Roosevelt, over the head in the campaign. Besides, could the islands be bypassed successfully if a future invasion of Japan was needed? Was it worth the risk to Roosevelt? What about the potential slaughter of Filipinos, prisoners of war, and civilian internees, as had occurred by the Japanese in China? MacArthur in the Waikiki debate was eloquent and passionate about the troops he had left behind and the civilian internees and the brave Filipinos who were very loyal to America.

After several hours during which Nimitz and MacArthur had argued their strategies, Roosevelt proposed a drive around Honolulu in an open-top convertible to see where the war had started, and of course, to be seen and photographed. He sat between Nimitz and MacArthur looking, smiling, and waving. After the excursion, and noting the body language of Roosevelt and MacArthur, Nimitz is reported to have said quietly to an aide: "I think I lost the debate." The next day, Roosevelt told the military leaders that the Philippines would be liberated in as expeditious a manner as possible, and MacArthur would command that attack. Nimitz was tasked with continuing his cross-Pacific island-hopping attack as well.

Liberation

Manila
January 31, 1945

The classic assault on the capital of Manila, taught at the War
College, is through Lingayen Gulf, about 110 miles northwest of the city, and halfway down the western side of Luzon
Island. It was the route followed by the Japanese in late 1941,
and the route for the final phase of the plan selected by Douglas
MacArthur to liberate the country. Some 850 ships arrived in
the gulf early in January 1945, but it was nearly February before the Army's 1st Cavalry Division arrived on Luzon from
Leyte Gulf. There had been rumors that the Japanese, most
likely the Imperial Navy or Marines, were planning on slaugh-
tering the internees in Santo Tomas. MacArthur met with the
division commander, Maj. Gen. Verne D. Mudge, and urged
him into a lightning thrust into the capital to save the prisoners in Santo Tomas.

"Go around the Nips; bounce off the Nips, but go to Manila.
Free the internees at Santo Tomas," he told Mudge.

The division commander formed two flying columns, each
with 700 cavalry troops, a tank company, a battery of 105mm
howitzers, and enough support vehicles to carry the soldiers and
supplies. As the flying columns hurried south, Marine Corps
dive bombers flew overhead, scouting and bombing, and then
over-flew the camp at Santo Tomas. One of the planes dropped

a small package with the message inside: "Roll out the barrel. Santa Claus is coming Sunday or Monday."

The soldiers of the 1st Cavalry drove hard, using motorized transport while the other designated division, the Army's 37th Infantry, tasked with entering Manila with the "First Cav" along their flank, was advancing partially on foot. By Saturday, February 3, the first tanks rolled through the Santo Tomas University main gate and liberation was at hand. It was about nine o'clock at night, but nobody in Santo Tomas was sleeping. Some hours earlier, nearly 50 Japanese soldiers occupied the Education Building, holding the internees inside as hostages. After entry of the Americans and a tense few hours, negotiators worked out a deal where the Japanese soldiers were allowed to keep their weapons and were driven by truck out of the camp into Manila in return for releasing the hostage internees.

Days after the arrival of the 1st Cavalry, Bob and Naomi wrote home February 6 on Red Cross stationery to her folks: "We are all four well and you have probably already been notified. *[Not, it turned out, for another two weeks.]* We will all be coming home at the first available opportunity and believe it will be very soon."

They continued: "You have never seen such joy and demonstrations as there have been here since the Americans came into camp. No Army-Navy football demonstration ever equaled the one that followed the arrival of those first tanks on Saturday night. We are still a little dazed with it all, and especially with the fact that we can have all we want to eat again." Later, they concluded: "It all seems like a glorious dream from which we're afraid we will awaken."

"And so we come to Saturday February 3, 1945," Mary Alice recalled, "… and what a Saturday night it was. About mid-day, several planes with U.S. markings flew quite low over the camp. Goggles were thrown from one of them with a note reading … 'Roll out the barrel … will be in today or tomorrow.' Can you think of any sweeter words?

"Gun fire … artillery … mortars … the clanking of tanks, machine gun fire … all these were heard in the distance. But were they ours … or theirs? No one knew. The Japanese ordered everyone inside the building and scurried around the area in front, setting up concealed machine gun barricades. At about 8:45 p.m. that night, with everyone holding their collective breath in the dark, there were sounds outside the walls and the unmistakable sound of an American voice shouting: '… where the hell is the gate?'"

Years later, Mary Alice still remembered the names of two of the tanks breaking through the gate: 'Battling Basic' and 'Georgia Peach.'

As the tanks pulled up in front of the building, "an officer climbed out and said a simple … 'hello, folks.' And pandemonium broke loose," Mary Alice recalled. "Internees surged out of the building – stupidly perhaps in view of the on-going rifle fire – but certainly understandably. This was the day we had waited three long years for … the end of our captivity."

Unfortunately, this was not the end. In fact, it was just the beginning of the battle for Manila, a fight which would virtually destroy much of the city and kill at least 100,000 Filipinos, many summarily executed by the Japanese as "guerillas."

Shelling began across the city, and the internment camp was not immune. In fact, it seemed that some of the Japanese guns positioned in Fort William McKinley were zeroed in on the camp. First small and then larger shells fell in the university grounds, hitting the main building and even some of the shanty areas.

Many people took shelter in the stairs and landings of the big concrete structures and on the main corridor leading into the front of the admin building. Some reports put the death toll in the camp from the shelling at 15, with another 40 or so wounded. Mary Alice Foley, a teenager of about 19, had volunteered to help as a hospital aide to the army nurses in the infirmary, carrying bedpans and instruments, bandages, or anything that was required. "I later saw a report," she said, "that the floors of the main building were slippery with blood. It is my strongest memory of those days. I was working in the emergency area, and the only way I could keep my sanity while walking over blood was to keep reminding myself not to slip and fall carrying the supplies."

The fight for the city continued, and so did the shelling. It is always surprising afterwards to note what people do in times of stress. Many in the camp in the days before the 1st Cavalry arrived had been on the verge of starvation, eating only boiled rice once a day. For many, it was a chore even to climb the stairs from the ground floor up to their first-floor sleeping rooms, having to stop to rest several times on the way up, they were so emaciated. The Americans had brought food to the internees, in a quality and quantity they hadn't seen in years. Breakfast was served and people sat outside eating while artillery explosions rocked various parts of the university grounds or in the surrounding neighborhood. They didn't duck or take cover. They bent over their bowls and finished what they were eating.

Several days later, the outdoor movie screen was again put into use. The film, Mary Alice recalled, was "Rhapsody in Blue," the bio-pic of George Gershwin. The screen was out in the open air and behind it there were shells exploding. "I was watching the movie, seeing and hearing shells whiz over my head and thinking 'no one will ever believe this!'"

Western Union brought a telegram to the Bishop home in Delaware, dated February 20, 1945: "Am pleased to inform you that information indicates the rescue by our forces of Robert E Senior Naomi Bishop Robert B Junior and William G Smith physical conditions good Formerly interned at Santo Tomas (Stop) You may send free through American Prisoner of War Information Bureau this office one only twenty five word message. (Stop) Signed Lerch Provost Marshal General."

Madge

February 10, 1945

Although the 1st Cavalry had arrived days before, the camp continued for several days to be subject to random artillery shelling. The city was a battleground, and the U.S. Army troops in Santo Tomas were as cut off from the main body of the army early on as the internees. Red Cross workers had come in shortly after the troops with medical supplies and food, but there was still danger everywhere.

Madge Gelbwaks had her bed in the Annex not far from Naomi and the boys. Her children were older, nine and eleven, both girls. She had been matron of honor in Naomi's wedding in 1939, and they remained close.

"It's probably worse now than before the Army came in," Madge said to Naomi. "What with the shelling ... you can't tell when one of the things will explode over your head or somewhere."

"Yes. I try to keep the boys inside, but it's hard. They're better off with the building around them, I think."

Madge agreed. She was keeping her children in as well.

"When it started," Madge said, "I use to crouch next to the walls and scurry here and there. But what the hell. If they're going to get you ... they'll get you! Now I just go about my business. Screw them!"

Naomi smiled and nodded. They had to go outside to get 'chow' ... Red Cross and Army food ... but still it was better to stay inside as much as possible, she thought.

They spent much time trying to figure out a pattern to the shelling. It wasn't even clear if the Japanese or the Americans were doing the shooting. For sure, sometimes the shots were accidents, but it seemed at other times they were planned. Nothing seemed to coincide with anything they could plan on to reduce the risk.

Late in the afternoon, one of the other women in the Annex came hurrying in.

"Madge has been hit," she said. "Shrapnel. Hit her in the face. She's down in the infirmary."

Naomi asked the woman to watch the boys and made her way through the crowd of women, down to the care station.

Madge was lying in a bed, the middle of her face covered in a bandage, blood visible through the white cotton. She grimaced a sort of smile at Naomi.

"How are you doing?" Naomi asked.

"They gave me some morphia. It's starting to hurt less."

"What happened?"

"I was walking to the latrine and a shell exploded nearby. They tell me it hit my nose. Took part of it off."

"Oh, my word," Naomi said.

"It could have been worse," Madge said, thinking of the two women killed near her. "Besides, I never liked the God damn thing anyway."

Mammy and Pappy

Santo Tomas
Late February 1945

Cpl. Bill Gawthorp was a friend of Naomi's middle brother John T. Bishop and his wife, Geraldine (Mackey) Bishop. They had told the corporal about John's sister, a prisoner with her family in the Philippines. He remembered much of what John had told him as he fought through the South Pacific, except he forgot Naomi's first name and married name. Still, who knew? Maybe he would end up in the Philippines.

John Bishop, a graduate of the University of Delaware in 1936 with a degree in chemical engineering, spent the war in the greater Philadelphia area in defense work with the Phenolite Company and the National Vulcanized Fibre Company near Kennett Square, Pennsylvania. With one brother missing in action, a second brother in the Army, and a sister interned by the Japanese, he was exempted from joining the military and was doing important war work as well. He had married his sweetheart, Geraldine, called Jerry in the family, after Naomi had gone to the Philippines in 1939.

Cpl. Gawthorp had joined up in early 1942. He liked the Army and, after boot camp, was assigned to the Army's 37th Infantry. They landed in late January 1945 at Lingayen. He didn't know it, but the orders were for a desperate charge straight into Manila to free the prisoners in Santo Tomas. Douglas MacArthur had received intelligence that the Japanese were going to slaughter the internees before the Americans could arrive. Of course, he hadn't shared this with Cpl. Gawthorp, no doubt a bureaucratic oversight.

The flying drive on Manila by the 37th was tough and relentless. Gawthorp was part of the rear guard, sweeping up behind the quickly advancing troops. He was not in on the initial liberation of the camp by the 1st Cavalry. By the time he arrived, the Japanese had negotiated their withdrawal, and the camp was secure.

Tired and foot sore, the corporal approached the sentry at the entrance to the camp.

"Halt," the sentry said in a kind of bored way.

"I got to go in," Gawthorp said. "I want to visit some folks inside."

"You got a pass?"

"No."

"Well, you can't go in," the sentry said.

Bill Gawthorp stood and looked at him for a time, tired and dirty. He un-shouldered his carbine and cradled it in his hands. He had a funny look in his eyes.

"Listen," he said. "I got a mammy in heaven and a pappy in hell, and friends in Santo Tomas, and I'm gonna see one of them today."

The sentry looked carefully at the man in front of him, stepped back, and Cpl. Gawthorp walked into the camp. Actually, the corporal still didn't remember Naomi's first name or her married name. But in the camp, she had always used her full name, "Naomi Bishop Smith," and there weren't any other "Bishops" interned in Santo Tomas. Cpl. Gawthorp found the Smiths after a time and spent part of the afternoon chatting about home. Naomi a couple of weeks later wrote to her parents in Laurel: "He is a nice chap and we certainly did enjoy his visit."

They saw the corporal again some ten days later and Naomi wrote to her brother John telling him his friend Bill was "well and looked good."

The Fly-By

Late February, 1945

Lt. Col. Dick Ellis circled his B-25 twin engine Mitchell bomber over Manila Bay and headed toward Nicholas Field, just north of Fort William McKinley, near present-day Makati City just south of central Manila. The Japanese had fortified McKinley into one of the most concentrated fortifications in the Philippines, with Japanese Navy, Marine and Army units planning a last ditch stand against the Americans fighting to retake Manila, even removing guns from Japanese naval vessels to use against the allies. One wag had radioed: "Tell Halsey to stop looking for the Jap fleet. It's anchored on Nicholas Field." Even though the airfield had been retaken, there were artillery and mortar shells falling widely across the area.

Dick Ellis, a decorated air ace, although he was still shy of his 26th birthday, carefully set his twin tailed medium bomber on the pock marked runway, artfully dodging most of the craters. Although retaken by the Americans, the airfield was still in rough shape. He was group commander of the 90th Bombardment Squadron and had been in the United States Army Air Forces (USAAF) since his graduation from flight school in 1942.

Prior to attending college in 1941, Dick had been a student at Laurel's Central School. One of his teachers had been Naomi Bishop. His mother, Elsie, had written him that "Miss Bishop" was an internee in Manila at Santo Tomas. Could Dick look in on her and see how she was doing? The Ellis family had been close neighbors of the Bishops in Laurel for years. Being near in age, only three or four years apart, Dick Ellis, John Bishop, and Billy Bishop knew each other quite well. And Laurel was a small town.

Dick commandeered a Jeep and had himself driven to Santo Tomas from the airfield. He had a mission to complete. Of course, he spent some happy time with Naomi and met Bob and the two children when he got to the camp, with much talk of home and how everyone was faring. But then, after a time, he sat quietly alone with Naomi in the shanty and told her about her brother, Bill. First Lt. James William Bishop, United States Army Air Forces, (USAAF) had been reported missing in action on December 5, 1942. A bomber pilot flying B-25s, just like Dick Ellis, he had been reported missing after a mission near Bizerte, Tunisia, in northwest Africa. On December 5, 1943, the Army declared him officially killed. He had trained in England, serving for one year eleven months, and was decorated with the Purple Heart. It was the first Naomi had heard of her brother since her parents decided not to add to her burdens with the news of Billy.

She wrote home in March a couple of weeks later: "We have seen Dick twice this week *(March 8, 1945)* and it has been a real treat. Tell Elsie he looks fine."

She continued: "He told us about Bill, and while it was a blow, it was not totally unexpected because you all hadn't mentioned the boys *[Bill and George, who part of the time had been serving in the War Department in Washington, D.C.]* in the letter you wrote Thanksgiving Day. Bill was at least doing what he wanted to do and that is some consolation for it could have been much worse than it was this way."

Dick Ellis visited the Smiths at the camp again later and offered Bob a chance to fly over Manila in Ellis' B-25, a fly-by. It was a treat, although the fighting had done major damage to the city, once called "The Pearl of the Orient." More than 100,000 Filipinos were killed in the Japanese door-to-door battle to keep the Americans out. It stood in stark contrast to the decision by

MacArthur to declare Manila an open city in 1941, no doubt saving countless lives then. Returning to Nicholas Field with Bob, Dick Ellis landed on the damaged runway. He hit one pothole just as he was stopping and blew out a tire, nonchalantly telling the ground crew to replace it as he left the plane, much to Bob's amusement.

Lt. Col. Ellis after the war returned to university, completing his studies, but then rejoined the U.S. Air Force. He ultimately became a four-star general and head of the Strategic Air Command.

My Captain

The *U.S.S Admiral Capps,* a 20,000-ton Navy troop transport painted standard Navy gray, left San Francisco on February 21, 1945 for Hollandia, New Guinea, with about 3,500 troops on board. It later departed New Guinea for the Philippines after delivering its troops and arrived March 20, 1945 at Leyte. Next it sailed to Manila and picked up its "passengers" via ship's tender (an LST) since the docks were wrecked, leaving April 8 for San Francisco. George Bishop in Laurel received a telegram on April 4 informing him that the Smiths "were en-route to the United States from the Philippines."

Naomi had been packing and repacking what little they had since they were put on notice that they would be leaving "soon." She was actually trying to decide what to throw away, but they had so little she finally took it all. No specific departure time was given, and they were told they might have to leave at a moment's notice. That was almost exactly what happened. With only an hour's notice, they were taken, along with several dozen others, by truck from Santo Tomas to the port of Manila, where they boarded an LST for transfer to the *Admiral Capps* anchored in Manila Bay. Other trucks came over the next few hours, discharging former internees from several camps for boarding. Neither Bob nor Naomi ever saw the university, Manila, or the Philippines again.

Several days out from Manila en route to San Francisco, Naomi had gotten an appointment to the beauty parlor that had been set up below decks by the Navy for the women internees being repatriated home. "I haven't gotten my hair done professionally in three years," she said to Bob. "Watch the boys. I may be a couple of hours!" She beamed and left him standing with the two boys. They went up on deck to play in a playground the Navy had set up for the kids.

He wasn't the captain. In fact, he was a simple ward steward who wore a white uniform without any markings except shoulder identification. But to Bobby, he was in charge of the whole ship. He would play with some of the children, under orders to keep them safe and occupied ... as only the Navy could do.

About an hour and a half later, one of the women going into the beauty parlor mid-decks, who knew Naomi slightly, stopped her on her way out. "Oh," she said. "How is Bobby? I hope it isn't serious."

Naomi headed to the ship infirmary, hurrying ... and worrying. Bobby was sitting on a metal exam table, a Navy pharmacist mate finishing putting a plaster on his forehead. "How is he?" she asked scooping him up into her arms. Bobby clung to her, his blue eyes still wet from tears.

Bob stood at the side, holding Billy's hand. "What happened?" she asked.

Sheepishly, he explained. Bobby had been playing and then across the deck he saw "my captain, my captain." He waved and then ran straight over to him. Unfortunately, the swings set up by the Navy were in between them and in full use. One swing with a little girl aboard clipped Bobby as he ran to the steward. He went down like he'd been pole axed.

Naomi waited until they had walked out of the infirmary. "Three years ... through a war ... and shelling ... and gunfire ... and battles ... I've kept them in one piece. Now I ask you to watch them for an hour, and I come out to this!" she said.

108

He looked at her and slightly shrugged his shoulders. What could you say?

She looked at him. "Honestly!" she said slowly, shaking her head. And they walked back to their cabin area ... together as they had done everything.

The *Admiral Capps* docked in late April at the Embarcadero in San Francisco. The Red Cross was waiting, taking the internees to the Civic Auditorium, where they had facilities to provide people with clothes, some money, documents to get them hotel accommodations, and a warm "welcome home." Also, there were telegrams from family for many internees. One was awaiting Naomi from the Bishops. The April notification telegram had given contact information in San Francisco and various ways to provide additional money beyond the limited cash the Red Cross dispensed to help them get home.

Aussie Bastard

San Francisco
Late April 1945

"Thank God for the Red Cross," Naomi often said afterwards. They were on hand when the *Admiral Capps* docked at Pier 32, just down from the Ferry Building in San Francisco. They took charge. Families had priority, so even though war conditions made hotel space scarce, the Red Cross had found the Smiths a room in a moderate hotel just off Market Street, on O'Farrell. Although raised in Los Angeles, Bob knew San Francisco well, having graduated from Stanford University south of the city on the Peninsula.

They had little to wear. The Red Cross right away had provided some clothes, a coat for each of the boys and one for Naomi, which she dearly appreciated in the cool San Francisco April afternoon. She thought of the Mark Twain comment: "The coldest winter I ever spent was one summer in San Francisco." The boys had shorts and T-shirts. Bob had been given surplus mixed army gear, with the insignia removed, an Australian short jacket, and U.S. fatigue pants. Their new duffle contained two sets of underwear, some toiletries, toothbrushes and paste, and Billy's stuffed teddy bear, made by Madge one Christmas early in the war.

They settled in the hotel, giving the desk clerk the voucher from the Red Cross.

Bob put in a telephone call to his mother, May, in Los Angeles, collect. It took 20 minutes for the call to go through. Naomi placed a collect call home to Laurel, Delaware.

The circuits were tied up, and the call could not be completed. Besides, it was after nine at night back east, so she booked a call for the morning.

Meanwhile, the two boys were fascinated by the flush toilet in the hotel, so different from the shipboard system, and unlike anything in the camp. Naomi heard the flushing, once, twice, and again and again, and smiled. And then it got quiet, a sure sign of trouble. She went into the bathroom. The toilet was running, water swirling around the bowl. It didn't stop. She motioned the boys to the side and lifted the tank lid.

The flushing mechanism was broken. She called Bob, who looked at it and called the desk clerk. It was fixed within the hour. Rules were set up for flushing in the future.

It was early, but they were tired and hungry, so they left the hotel to find "chow," their first meal in the U.S. The Red Cross had given Bob $8, a food allotment for the two days. It was all they had, except some worthless Japanese pesos from Manila. The coffee shop at the corner was crowded, but they soon got a place. The boys wanted rice.

As a treat Naomi ordered Coca Cola for them. It fizzed up their noses, and they didn't like it. Bob had a chicken fried steak, and Naomi liver and bacon. It was heaven. After the meal, with numerous cups of coffee, they left the shop and walked along Market Street, reluctant to return to the hotel.

The street was crowded and busy. Bob held Bobby by the hand and walked slightly ahead of Naomi, who was carrying Billy. Loud music came out of a bar and two Marines, seriously drunk, stumbled out of the joint, one bumping into Bob.

"Watch it, Mac," one said.

"Aussie bastard," the other said, looking at the combat jacket Bob was wearing.

"Let's show the son of a bitch how he should walk when he's in America," the first said. He squared off, ready for a fight. Naomi came up to Bob's side.

"I'm not Australian." he said. "They gave us these things on the ship."

"Why?"

"We didn't have anything," Bob said. The Marines looked at each other. "We were released from Santo Tomas Internment Camp in Manila."

"We were there over three years," Naomi said. The Marines looked from one to the other, and then focused on the two children.

"Jesus, we're sorry, man." He stuck out his hand and Bob took it.

"Come on, Tommy," one Marine said to the other. They got down on their knees and dug into their pockets, pulling out all the money they had, change mostly, and piled it on the sidewalk. In a minute, the one called Tommy scooped it up and gave it to Bob.

"No," he said, "You don't have to …"

"Naw, take it for the kids. Buy them some toys."

"Jesus, we're sorry," the one said.

"Welcome home," Tommy said. They smiled and shook Bob's hand again, the two then stumbling off up Market Street, weaving into the crowd and disappearing. At the Woolworth store nearby, Naomi let the boys each pick out two toys. There was still nearly four dollars from the change left over.

Back at the hotel, Bob's mother had wired them money for tickets for the train to Los Angeles. They left the next morning. Bobby forgot one of his toys in the hotel and there were tears until the novelty of the train faded the memory.

From Los Angeles, after a few days with Bob's family … his mother, sister Edith, younger brother LeRoy, his Aunt Ione and Uncle Johnny Rodgers … they traveled east to Philadelphia, where George and Annie Bishop met them at the train station and drove the family south to their home in Laurel. Naomi, after a few days' rest, was asked to give a talk about her experiences to the workers in the DuPont war plant near Wilmington, since the war was still going. She did it. Her "war work," she would call it, and then, some weeks later, it was all over. The war had ended and life became "normal" again.

The End

Tokyo Bay
September 1945

The "Proceedings," as General Douglas MacArthur called them, took place aboard the battleship *USS Missouri* at anchor in Tokyo Bay.

Representatives of the Allied fighting nations, Brits, Aussies, Canadians, the Dutch, New Zealanders, the Chinese, Americans, and many others, were gathered on the decks and super structure of the battle ship, thousands of men in various uniforms. The whole thing was choreographed by that fine showman, Douglas MacArthur.

Representatives of the government and military of the Empire of Japan filed aboard the ship to sign the Articles of Surrender. The ceremony was surprisingly brief, considering that representatives of all the warring nations had to sign the surrender documents.

After all had signed, Gen. MacArthur took the microphone. "These proceedings are closed," he announced, and all departed to their tasks.

Standing high on the upper deck of the battleship, Col. George Bishop, the one-time army lieutenant and brother whom Naomi had traveled half-way around the world to visit in 1937, watched as the ceremonies unfolded. As with others, the colonel received a photocopy of the Articles of Surrender, which he showed to

Bob and Naomi in California two years later. He gave them a copy which they kept until the end of their lives. After the war, George retired in 1946 from the army and settled in Las Vegas, Nevada. He died in Santa Barbara, California in 1954.

Often in the years after the war, Naomi would say: "If there's another war, I plan to spend it in Kansas." The family settled in California.

Philippine Commonwealth President Manuel Quezon on left,
Lt. George Bishop and his sister Naomi at 1937 Manila reception.

The Fall Annual Sales meeting of Glo-Co in Manila, taken in 1939 just two months after Naomi and Bob, seated in front row with office and administrative staff, were married.

Sikia Apartments on Avenue M.H. del Pilar street view in 1941.

The amah Kong with Bobby, about three months,
at the rear of the Sikia Apartments in Manila in the summer of 1941.

Picture of the Smith's shanty in the camp, with Bobby and Billy sitting on the steps.
Photo is blurry since the Catholic priest who took it buried the film for nearly a year.

Bobby and Billy at the shanty.

The two boys playing (and posing for the camera) outside the shanty.

Bobby wandering near the shanty.

SPECIAL PASS No.83

NAME: Mr. R. E. Smith
FROM: Shanty Area C.18
TO: Main Building and
     return
TIME: At all hours during
      air raids
DUTY: Head Pharmacist.

For: INTERNEE
     COMMITTEE

For: COMMAN-
     DANT.

Special pass to allow Bob Smith to travel from the Main Building around the campus during air raids.

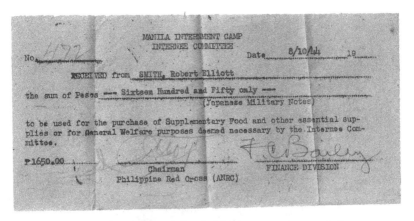

*Receipt for funds given by the Red Cross in Manila to Bob
to secure supplies as approved by the Internee Committee.*

*War time Japanese issued currency used in Philippines.
There were various denominations.*

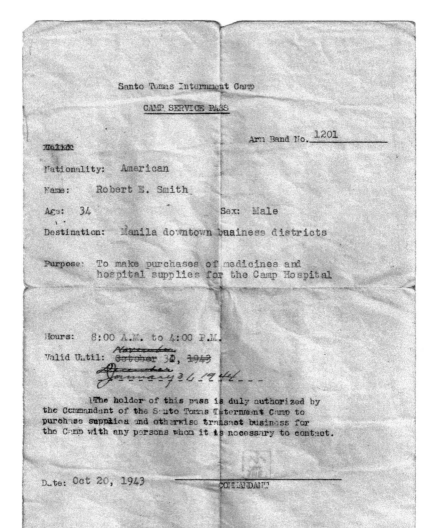

Santo Tomas Internment Camp

CAMP SERVICE PASS

Arm Band No. 1201

~~Walker~~

Nationality: American

Name: Robert E. Smith

Age: 34   Sex: Male

Destination: Manila downtown business districts

Purpose: To make purchases of medicines and
          hospital supplies for the Camp Hospital

Hours: 8:00 A.M. to 4:00 P.M.

Valid Until: ~~October~~ 3~~0~~, ~~1943~~
November
January 26, 1944

        The holder of this pass is duly authorized by
the Commandant of the Santo Tomas Internment Camp to
purchase supplies and otherwise transact business for
the Camp with any persons whom it is necessary to contact.

Date: Oct 20, 1943   COMMANDANT

*Pass for Bob to travel from the camp to "downtown business districts"
to make purchases of hospital supplies for the camp.*

MANILA INTERNMENT CAMP
Internee Committee
Finance and Supply Department

No. 1.92

Date 8/10/44

RECEIVED from SMITH, Robert Elliott   C-18
                     (Name)   (Address)
— By order of the Japanese Military Authorities —

Pesos — Nine Hundred —   P900.00

for deposit in the Bank of Taiwan, Manila Branch, in the Individual
Internee Deposits Account, in the name of the Chairman, Internee
Committee, subject to withdrawals as may be permitted by the Japanese
Military Authorities.

Specimen Signature
   of Depositor

                                                Finance Division

(This Receipt to be surrendered on delivery of "Pass Book")

Receipt for funds deposited by Bob in the Bank of Taiwan as required by the Japanese in late summer 1944, when they confiscated assets of internees after the Imperial Army took over management of the camp. The action severely curtailed the ability of internees to get goods from the local economy.

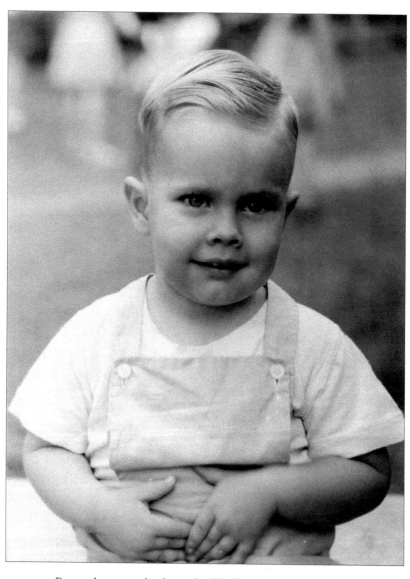

*Reported propaganda photo taken by the Imperial Army in 1944
at the camp of Bobby, then a little over three years old.*

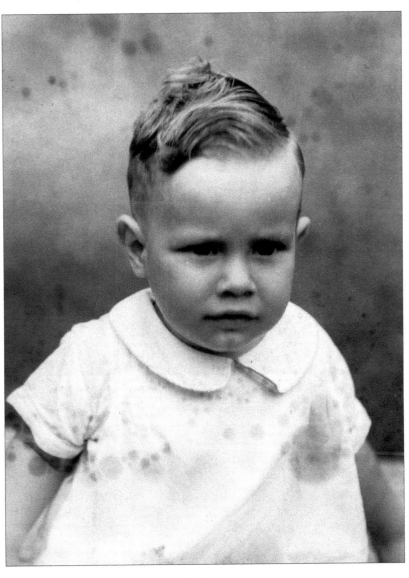

Propaganda photo of Billy, taken at the same time,
then just under two years of age. No proof photos were used by Japanese.

George Bishop Senior, Annie Bishop and James William Bishop
at home in Laurel Delaware in early 1941 when Billy joined the army.

James William Bishop

*Billy (left), Naomi, Bobby and Bob arrive in San Francisco in 1945
aboard the USS Admiral Capps, delighted to be home.*

*Col. George Bishop, center with mustache, in Tokyo following
1945 surrender ceremonies aboard the battleship USS Missouri.*

Afterwards

Bob and Naomi

Bob immediately began his search for work. His old company in Manila, Glo-Co, was on very rocky ground financially and had virtually ceased to exist. Besides, who wanted to go back now? He received a very heartwarming letter from Teddy Roque in Manila, one of the Glo-Co staff, referencing both Jesus Leonides and Joe Sta. Teresa, asking: "… don't you want to be with us? Or back in the Philippines …"

Bob sent a friendly note in reply, but he and Naomi were not leaving the U.S. He talked with some companies in Philadelphia, as well as DuPont in Wilmington, while visiting the Bishops. But he also contacted friends in California. Bob was a Westerner at heart and really preferred something back West. A Stanford friend, Marshall Mustain, worked for the Standard Oil Company of California (years later renamed Chevron) in San Francisco. He got Bob a job interview, and Bob was offered a job at the Richmond Refinery, a lab tech 6, bottom of the ladder, but on the ladder at least. He was with Chevron for some 30 years, rising to chief chemist at Richmond and, in the last two years before retirement, refinery manager at Bakersfield.

Naomi got a job as a substitute school teacher until Billy started school, and then she taught full-time for the next nearly 20 years, retiring happily in the mid-1960s. Naomi's father, George, died in 1948, and her mother some 20 years later moved to California and lived with Bob and Naomi until she died at age nearly 90 in 1972.

Frank and Ella

The Foleys returned to New York, ultimately buying a home in Great Neck, Long Island, where Frank learned (finally) to drive a car. Frank went to work for his old firm, which had been rebuilt after the hiatus of bankruptcy, commuting to the city each day.

His friend and mentor, the owner of the firm, died, and the company had been taken over by his son. Frank and the son did not see the world the same way. One Sunday after church, Frank was paging through the *New York Times* and saw an advertisement looking for an experienced trader in New York, "familiarity with jute-hemp and Asia" considered "highly desirable." After some thought, Frank wrote a letter of inquiry to the post office box in the ad. A few days later, his boss called him in. "So you're looking for a job?" he asked Frank, who hemmed and hawed a bit. The boss took out Frank's letter, showed it to him, and fired him on the spot. "Frank Foley is the only man I ever knew who applied for his own job," Bob used to say.

After some months of looking, Frank was offered a job at the U.S. Post Office in Great Neck. At that time, Bob and Naomi and the boys were visiting Naomi's mother in Delaware and decided to drive up to Long Island "on the way home to the Bay Area." As was usual, they didn't contact the Foleys until they had checked into a local Long Island motor lodge. Frank insisted that they come over right away. Sitting with a scotch in hand, Bob asked Frank what he was doing now.

"I'm working at the post office," he said.

"When did you start there?" Bob asked.

"Oh, today was my first day, but I called and told them my friends from Santo Tomas were in town ... so they gave me the day off." He spent more than 25 years at the post office before retiring.

Ella resumed her life as a housewife. She was very active in the local Catholic church. Her only unrequited hope was for her only child to meet and marry a nice Catholic boy.

Mary Alice

Returning to New York with her parents, Mary Alice enrolled in the Katherine Gibbs Secretarial School, one of the pre-eminent schools of its kind in the country. After graduation, she went to work for a law firm in Long Island City, New York, and then several years later, joined International Business Machines World Trade organization in Manhattan. A highly professional executive secretary, after a number of years, she was offered the chance by IBM for an assignment with IBM Japan in Tokyo. It took some time to think through that "opportunity," but in the end she decided to take it. It was much more difficult for her mother, Ella, to come to terms with the idea. Mary Alice spent nearly three years in Tokyo at IBM. She said: "Working with the people in Tokyo was the best thing I could have done. It finally allowed me closure over what had happened."

She remained active in the Santo Tomas Internee Organization founded after the war. Her gentle prodding brought both Bob and Bill to the commemoration celebration of the 50th Anniversary of the Santo Tomas Liberation in 1995, held in Las Vegas. Living north of New York after retirement from IBM, she also became close with Bobby's son, Robert L. Smith, when he was a cadet at West Point, something she always treasured.

Bobby

After graduating from the University of California Berkeley, Bob joined the Air Force to fulfill his ROTC commitments during the Vietnam War. He liked the USAF, where he met his wife Judi LeBrun, an Elbow Lake, Minnesota native and Air Force nursing officer. He decided to make the USAF a career and spent nearly 30 years there, retiring as a full colonel. He was base commander at Whiteman Air Force base in Missouri prior to his last assignment at Vandenberg Air Force Base in California, from which he retired. Although he was urged several times by Naomi, he never reached out to Dick Ellis, then a USAF four-star general, reluctant to be seen as "brown nosing"—a decision he said in later life that he regretted, always curious about Dick's memories of the Philippine experience.

After retirement, Bob became director of elections for Santa Barbara County, a job he held for nearly a decade and a half. He and Judi retired to North Carolina. They have three children, Jennifer, Emily, and Robert, and (at last count) seven grandchildren.

Billy

After graduating from Stanford University, Bill began work as a newspaper reporter for *The Salt Lake Tribune.* He met his wife, Irene Carson, from Oshawa, Ontario, Canada, in the Utah capital, where they became ski buddies and soul mates. In 1968, he returned to school, graduating with an MBA from Columbia University in the City of New York, where he and Mary Alice became fast friends (she was the first person he told about his marriage proposal to Irene and her acceptance). Irene and Bill had one daughter, Elizabeth, who lived in Buffalo, New York, working in a PhD program there. He worked for some two decades at the General Electric Co., traveling often to Asia (Hong

Kong, Japan, China, Singapore, and Malaysia), and returning several times to Manila and visiting Santo Tomas. Irene
worked as a paralegal until her retirement. Bill still does con-
sulting work with a China-based consumer products company called Intex in their Long Beach, California office, owned
by a Chinese-American entrepreneur. He and Irene moved to
Las Vegas, Nevada in 1998, where they lived happily ever after. *(An ironical note: When Bill was a sophomore at Stanford, his
roommate, assigned by the university, was Ben Haraguchi, a California
Japanese-American, born at Tanforan Race Track, en route to a desert
internment center established for Japanese-Americans by the Roosevelt
Administration. Ben spent his first years, like Bill, in internment.)*

Lt. James William Bishop

The Bishops had received two "official" notifications from the
U.S. government regarding their youngest son, called Billy, in
the family. First, they were notified in 1942 that he was "missing in action." Then a year later, with no new information coming to the Army, they were informed December 5, 1943, as required under federal law, that he had been "killed in action,"
just about six weeks shy of his 27th birthday. George Bishop
was active in local Laurel and Sussex County politics, holding
a number of minor positions at various times, but despite con-
tacting anyone he could think of, from Delaware's two sena-
tors to others, he was unable to find out more about "his boy."

In November 1943, a month before the Army Air Corps had
informed him officially of Billy's death, George Bishop received a
letter from Mrs. Ethel Keeler of Long Beach, California. She was
the sister of Billy's co-pilot 2nd Lt. Donald Oliphant on the mission on which he went missing. Photos of the letter are printed below. It is the only "explanation" the Bishops ever received about
what happened.

Nov. 28, 1943

Dear Mr. Geo. Bishop:

I am the eldest sister of Lieut. Donald Oliphant and as I have devoted considerable time trying to find some clue of my brother and those who were with him on Dec. 5, 1942, Don's mother and father thought that I could more fully answer your letter in response to their letter to you.

I shall relate to you the information we have and the order in which it was received.

On Dec. 17th we received the telegram "missing in action".

On Feb. 5th we received a letter from the Group commander which contained this information:

"The information we have is briefly this. Donald along with others of our Group were engaged in an important bombing mission some distance behind the enemy's front line. The bombing had been completed successfully and the plane in which he was serving was noticed to be losing altitude and pulling away from the formation. However, the ship appeared to be well under control. They were soon lost from view to the rest of the formation and did not return to the base."

About two months ago I read in the paper that a bomber pilot had returned to Inglewood from North Africa---Lieut. Robert Cunningham. So I went to his home to see him but he was out so his mother took my phone number and address. His mother informed me that he was in the 310th Bomber Group but of another squadron, had gone across at about the same time that my brother had gone across, but she did not know whether or not he knew my brother. The next morning the phone rang and Bob (the above mentioned pilot) said yes, he knew Donald and was with him on that mission of Dec. 5th but in another plane and could give me the details of that mission. He said, "Keep up your hope. There is a good chance he is safe. Don't give up hope." Several days later he came to my home and told me about Dec. 5th. I had several maps laid out and Bob traced the line of flight on a map on page 20 of April 26th 1943 issue of Life Magazine. Below is a sketchy tracing.

134

This is what Bob told me. On or about Nov. 11th the boys landed in
Casablanca. They were without food or shelter. Neither the infantry or
navy had extra supplies for the air group. They finally got some tomato
juice and subsisted on it until the army took them in. They had been sent from
England with instructions to merely watch and learn for about two months before
going into action. Their commanding officer was to come later and superintend
actual operations. To the surprise of the Allies the battles turned against
them and every available man was thrown into battle. As result our boys, without
maintenance crews or actual battle experience, were ordered into combat. As
their high ranking officers had not arrived, our boys had to plan their missions,
load and service their planes, in fact do everything. They went to Algeria
and were quartered there. From Algeria they went on a mission to bomb troop
concentrations at Gabes. In planning their mission of Dec. 5th they were up
all the previous night loading and servicing their planes, checking their flight
plans and their secret agent reports at Bizerta. Their plan was to bomb the
airfield at Bizerte the morning of Dec. 5th, and this they were able to do.
They set out from Algeria and flew up a valley from the south toward Ferryville.
Contrary to their previous information, anti-aircraft fire was heavy throughout
this valley. Flying at an altitude of 8,000 feet they arrived at Ferryville at
11:00 A.M. Dec. 5th and turned west for their run over the airfield outside
Bizerte. Just at this time, four blazes of gunfire were seen at Bizerte, one
shot striking our boy's plane. One engine was hit and began smoking and the
plane began losing altitude but remained under control and continued on its
course. Here is the formation of our planes:

(diagram of plane formation with handwritten notes: "← Bob's plane. Bob an observer." and "← Bill and Don's plane.")

Our seven B-25's had a cover of six P-38 fighter planes. Anti-aircraft fire
was terrific from Bizerte. At times the smoke from bursting anti-aircraft
shut our planes off from each other's sight. German fighter planes arose
from the airfield and engaged our planes. Bob saw the guns on our plane blazing
away furiously at the German fighters.

Our boy's plane was last seen about 20 to 25 miles west of Bizerte on the
line of flight as it was lost to sight behind a sand dune on the coast west of
the town of Bizerte. Bob estimated the plane to be about 50 feet above the
ground when last seen. The plane landed in a sandy area which is considered
by flyers to be the safest place for a forced landing. A P-38 pilot and the
pilot of the plane next to our boys both saw the plane just before it went
behind the dune and they both feel it had a good chance for a safe landing.
In fact they were so sure the plane made a safe landing, that at Christmas
time they speculated on where our boys might be spending Christmas.

The next morning after the mission, a reconnaisance plane was sent over
that area. There was no plane to be seen, only a long streak in the sand where
a plane made a landing, numerous wheel tracks and foot prints. No plane parts
were seen nor no smudge such as a burning plane would make. As a highway runs
along this coast leading to Bizerte, it was thought the Germans came out and
got this plane as it was one of the first B-25's to fall into their hands in
this area, and perhaps the men were taken in for questioning.

About six months ago we received Don's billfold containing his identification cards and picture. This was sent by his quartermaster. Have you received your son's?

As Bob knows your son, Bill, I wonder if you would like to have Lieut. Cunningham's address. Lieut. Robert Cunningham, 4655 W. 64th St., Inglewood. He was on leave at that time but has been reassigned. However, a letter to his home will be forwarded I am sure.

Bob knows only my brother and your son on our plane. He said there were five men on it. However, when I wrote to Washington, they sent the names of but four. We have now heard from you and the parents and families of the others and none of them have heard a thing. Here are the names and home addresses:

Mr. Geo. C. Bishop Laurel, Del.	Father of Lieut. James W. Bishop
Mr. Paul Hiers 614 Orangeburg St., Aiken, South Carolina	Brother of Staff. Sgt. William R. Hiers
Mr. Vernon March 633 35th St., Sacramento, Calif.	Father of Staff Sgt. Norman B. March
W. B. Oliphant 909 Hickory Street Santa Ana, Calif.	Father of Lieut. Donald Oliphant

Mr. Bishop, I have heard of a returned air force man who is hospitalized from North Africa and had been repatriated from a prison camp in France and I am writing to inquire if he knows any of our boys.

A brother of Don's has made inquiry through military police acquaintances and through the Red Cross in Algeria. If we get further information, will forward it on to you.

I regret the misfortune that has come to your family. I know of someone who may be able to give you some first-hand information as to your daughter's welfare in the Santo Tomas University Internment Camp. He is Dr. Claude Buss a former University of Southern California professor who was sent as a commissioner to Manilla, taken prisoner by the Japs and placed somewhat in charge of the Americans at Santos Tomas. His address: Dr. Claude Buss, c/o Dr. Polyzoides, International Relations Department, University of Southern California, Los Angeles, California. Dr. Buss in being repatriated from Japan on the S.S. Gripsholm and is to land in New York Dec. 1st.

Let us hear from you. We would like to know more about Bill. Perhaps we can exchange some snapshots.

Yours sincerely,

Mrs. Ethel Keeler

3816 Marron Avenue
Long Beach 7, California

The Rest of the Story on Billy Bishop

When developing the manuscript for this tale, the author showed a copy of it to his daughter, Elizabeth, a doctoral candidate in archeology at the State University of New York in Buffalo. She voluntarily undertook to research the missing flyer, 1st Lt. James William Bishop. The following is now-declassified information on the Army investigation as to what happened to the B-25 and its crew of four:

1st Lt. Billy Bishop was the pilot of the B-25 bomber, and 2nd Lt. Donald Oliphant was the co-pilot. Staff Sgt. William Hiers was the turret gunner, and Staff Sgt. Norman March was the bombardier. In November 1943, 11 months after the crew was listed as "missing in action," Donald Oliphant's brother, Army Lt. K.B. Oliphant, wrote to the Army seeking information about his brother, based on a copy of the same letter sent by his sister to George Bishop (noted above). The Army instituted an investigation, which was classified under normal practice as "Restricted" and "Confidential," as it was still wartime. The investigation documents, found by Elizabeth Smith in 2018, were declassified in 1973.

Following are key points from the multiple inquiries conducted by the Army Air Force at the time in North Africa:
- The principal question raised by the Oliphants was this: Did the B-25 "land in the sand dunes along the beach ... as reported by a reconnaissance plane" and were there indications of "removal from the dune" of such an aircraft? In summary, did the crew survive, and were they taken from the plane, and if so where? This was the story told by his family about the fate of Billy and the crew ... based on the Oliphant letter.
- One document of the Army 1943–44 inquiry was the December 5, 1942, USAAF Daily Operations Narrative. It states: "Eight B-25s of the 310th Bomb Op (m) took off from this base (Maison Blanche) to bomb the Sidi Ahmed Airdrome at

Bizerte, Tunisia. Six P-38s of the First Fighter Group acted as escorts. The B-25s bombed the airdrome hangars. Seven of the B-25s returned to this base. One B-25 failed to return. The plane was seen to be smoking as the formation left its target. The plane was seen to gradually lose altitude. At least one ME-109 was on its tail. The plane was last seen as it disappeared behind sand dunes about thirty miles west of the target along the beach between Cap Serrat and Cap Negro. No one actually saw this plane crash ..."

- In March 9, 1944, the inquiry report to senior Army brass notes: "Attention invited to 2nd and 3rd paragraphs of Oliphant's letter, which outlines certain details ..." The inquiry summary continues: "The information imparted by a 'young flying officer who just returned from North Africa' does not appear to have basis in fact ..."

- The report further notes: "Although previous search of the area between Cap Serrat and Cap Negro revealed no trace of the crash, another ground investigation was requested on 22 Feb. 44. Since travel is difficult due to terrain and weather conditions, part of the area must be covered on foot or on horseback ... Police officials, civic authorities, forest guards and native Arabs are being contacted to ensure compilation of all available evidence."

- Four days after the report to senior Army brass, March 13, 1944, the Criminal Investigation Division (CID) of the Office of the Provost Marshal issued a report: The report listed by name and function numerous French and Arab officials in the area whom they interviewed, as well as three French civilians and two sailors who lived or worked in the Cap Serrat area, as well as "numerous" shepherds and forest rangers.

- There was vivid recollection among the interviewed locals of a crash in January 1943 of an American plane into the sea near Cap Negro. All six Americans on board survived and were rescued by members of the Cap Negro naval patrol. Also reports of a mid-air crash November 10, 1942, of two English airplanes were investigated. The CID visited that site, reported to them by the French civilians. "The motors and parts of this plane were strewn about, although one tail assembly is practically intact." It was clear that the crash of any airplane, if observed, was well remembered by the locals and debris from crashes was noted by locals.

- The conclusion of the CID investigation was as follows: "Having exhausted every possible source from which any information could be obtained concerning this missing plane [Billy's and Don's aircraft] and its crew, and not being able to locate anyone who could shed any light on the subject, these agents have reached the conclusion that: a.) The plane in question could have fallen into the sea without anyone observing it; and b.) The reconnaissance plane reported to have seen the plane in question behind the hills could have observed the wreckage of planes referred to in paragraph 7 [the debris of the two English planes involved in the November mid-air crash] and readily mistaken and misidentified it."

- On March 15, 1944, the Adjutant General, Lt. Col. N.O. Thomas, concluded, in his report to the Commanding General XIIth Air Force: "It is believed by this headquarters that the plane crashed into the sea and neither the plane nor the bodies of the crew have been recovered."

The Delaware officials George Bishop contacted in 1943-1944 had no information from the Army on Billy's disappearance nor the Army investigation, although they asked. Likely that is because the reports were "classified" under wartime rules and held at XIIth Army in North Africa, and even more importantly, the Army had used Oliphant's brother's letter as the identification for the inquiry. All documents were therefore filed under "Oliphant," not "Bishop" in Army files. There is no record of the Army informing the Oliphant family of their inquiry conclusions, but if they did, likely the Oliphants were required to observe the classification of the reports.

- The North Africa American Cemetery and Memorial, Carthage, Tunis, Tunisia — on the Tablets of the Missing lists: 1st Lt. James William Bishop (24 Jan 1916–5 Dec 1942).

Also, his name is shown, in error, on the Becker County, Minnesota listing of the World War II Honor List of the Dead and Missing, ironically not too far from where Judi LeBrun, Bobby's wife, was raised.

George C. Bishop, the father of Billy, died in 1948; Annie Bishop, the mother, died in 1973; George H. Bishop, the brother, died in 1954. John T. Bishop, brother, died in 1967; Robert Smith, brother-in-law of Billy, died in 1979. Naomi Smith, sister, died in 1995. None were ever aware of the Army investigation documents.

EIN HERZ FÜR AUTOREN A HEART FOR AUTHORS À L'ÉCOUTE DES AUTEURS MIA KAPΔIA ΓΙΑ ΣΥΓΓ
HJÄRTA FÖR FÖRFATTARE UN CORAZÓN POR LOS AUTORES YAZARLARIMIZA GÖNÜL VERELIM S.
CUORE PER AUTORI ET HJERTE FOR FORFATTERE EEN HART VOOR SCHRIJVERS TEMOS OS AUT
SZÍVÜNK A SZERZŐINKÉRT SERCE DLA AUTORÓW EIN HERZ FÜR AUTOREN A HEART FOR AUTHORS À L'ÉCO
CORAÇÃO BCEЙ ДУШОЙ K ABTOPAM ETT HJÄRTA FÖR FÖRFATTARE À LA ESCUCHA DE LOS AUTО
AUTEURS MIA KAPΔIA ΓΙΑ ΣΥΓΓΡΑΦΕΙΣ UN CUORE PER AUTORI ET HJERTE FOR FORFATTERE EEN

The author

A former newspaper journalist, William Smith has worked and traveled extensively in Asia, Europe, and South America. He and his wife, Irene, a Canadian by birth, have lived and traveled throughout North America, living in various US states.

The publisher

He who stops getting better stops being good.

This is the motto of novum publishing, and our focus is on finding new manuscripts, publishing them and offering long-term support to the authors.
Our publishing house was founded in 1997, and since then it has become THE expert for new authors and has won numerous awards.

Our editorial team will peruse each manuscript within a few weeks free of charge and without obligation.

You will find more information about novum publishing and our books on the internet:

www.novumpublishing.com

CPSIA information can be obtained
at www.ICGtesting.com
Printed in the USA
LVHW081537130821
695245LV00003B/228